A Great American Tradition

KENTUCKY

The Chance of a Lifetime

DERBY

by Joe Hirsch and Jim Bolus

McGraw-Hill Book Company
New York St. Louis San Francisco Auckland Bogotá
Hamburg London Madrid Milan Mexico Montreal
New Delhi Panama Paris São Paulo Singapore
Sydney Tokyo Toronto

Printed and bound by Dai Nippon, Tokyo, Japan
Typeset by Dix Type, Inc., Syracuse, New York

Kentucky Derby® is used with the permission of Churchill
Downs Incorporated.

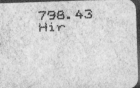

Library of Congress Cataloging-in-Publication Data
Hirsch, Joe.
Kentucky Derby.
Includes index.
1. Kentucky Derby, Louisville, Ky.   2. Kentucky Derby,
Louisville, Ky.—Pictorial works.   3. Louisville (Ky.)—
Description—Views.   I. Bolus, Jim.   II. Title.
SF357.K4H57   1987   798.4′3′0976944   87-27584

A Chanticleer Press Edition

Created and designed by Massimo Vignelli and Gudrun Buettner
Developed and edited by Susan Costello

Foreword by Eddie Arcaro
Caption essay by Dave Kindred

Contents

The authors are indebted to so many who have been of great assistance in the preparation and publication of this book. We wish to express our sincere thanks to Chanticleer Press for conceiving and producing *Kentucky Derby* and for their staunch support in every phase of this endeavor.

FINISH

We owe a great debt to President Tom Meeker, Vice President and General Manager Gerry Lawrence, Director of Media Relations Edgar Allen, Director of Admissions Joseph Westenhoefer, Director of Community Relations Mary Ann Cooper, Starter J.T. Wagoner, and stewards Bernard Hettel and Jack Middleton of Churchill Downs, who gave generously of their time and knowledge in providing much of the background for this book.

Doris Waren and Cathy Schenck of the Keeneland Library at Keeneland Race Course were extremely helpful in providing material, as was Theresa Fitzgerald of The Blood-Horse Library in Lexington, Kentucky.

Clifford Wickman, who retired January 1, 1988, as President of the Thoroughbred Racing Protective Bureau, also provided information, and we are grateful.

We very much appreciate the kind assistance of Jill Joseph of the Kentucky Derby Festival, Inc., who generously offered us her time and expertise.

The authors want to offer a special word of thanks to Eddie Arcaro, who graciously provided the foreword to this book, and who created so much Kentucky Derby history.

We wish to applaud the outstanding photographers who contributed to this book. A special acknowledgment is made to Jerry Cooke of *Sports Illustrated*, not only for his skilled work but for his valued advice. We are also grateful to Donna Lawrence and her associates for their support and guidance as well as for their photos.

To Cornelia Guest, whose editorial gifts and attention to detail are well displayed in the text, we owe a debt of thanks.

And finally, on a personal note, the authors wish to thank Suzanne Bolus for her many contributions to this book and the moral support she provided at all times.

When I was riding regularly in New York, in the 1940s and 1950s, our family lived in Garden City, not far from Belmont Park. My wife, Ruth, and I entertained from time to time, and while I would invite a lot of my racetrack pals and good customers, my wife usually invited many friends and neighbors who were not actively involved in racing.

My father was alive at the time, and after my mother died, he came up from Kentucky to live with us. He was a feisty little guy who always spoke his mind. Some years ago he ran a small handbook operation in Covington, Kentucky, across the river from Cincinnati, and there was a big sign in front of the place that read: ARCARO, BOOKMAKER.

A fellow from one of the national racing organizations asked my father to change the sign. He said it did not look good for the name of America's top jockey to be associated with bookmaking.

"Get him to change his name," my father said promptly. "I had it before he did. I'm not changing anything."

Anyway, we gave this party one evening and there must have been a hundred or more people in the house. On my way down to the party room in the cellar, I saw a professor from nearby Hofstra University backing my old man into a corner below the steps and talking to him with great enthusiasm. I couldn't help but overhear the conversation.

"Oh, Mr. Arcaro," the professor said. "You must be very proud of your son, making such a great name for himself as a jockey."

On and on he went, without drawing a deep breath, and I could see that my father had had about enough. As the professor reached a crescendo of praise, the old man looked at him and said, "Luckiest sonofabitch that ever lived. If he hadn't ridden Whirlaway, Citation, and those other Kentucky Derby winners, no one would ever have heard of him."

And, of course, he was so right. I was the luckiest guy that ever lived and the Kentucky Derby was a key factor. No matter where I've traveled, in this country, in Europe, anywhere, I don't think I've had five conversations with strangers that didn't include some question or comment about the Kentucky Derby. The Kentucky Derby may be the best-known horse race in the world, and it deserves that reputation because it is larger than life.

There is a story behind every running of the Derby, and some great revelry as well. Years ago, when everyone was young, I stayed out until 4:00 A.M. the night before the race, drinking and having a fine time. I got to sleep at the hotel about fifteen minutes before the big, burly Midwestern trainer Ben Jones phoned me and said he thought we ought to walk the track together to inspect the ground and talk strategy. I mumbled something about its sounding like a good idea, and he said he was sending a car around to pick me up.

"When?" I asked.

"In about ten minutes," he said, and hung up. Fifteen minutes later, I was still paralyzed by all the whiskey, and I was half asleep. With the morning sun beating down on Ben Jones and me, we slowly walked around the track. Every other inch of the mile, Jones stuck his heel in the ground to test the cushion, and he kept pointing out different things for me to watch for during the race. I didn't hear a word he said. After we were through I excused myself as gracefully as I could, headed for the jock's room, and went to sleep.

Fortunately, my horse, Lawrin, was at his best that day; we won the race, and I was off the hook. I don't know what kind of instructions Jones gave me, but after the race he roared to reporters: "That's my boy. Rode him exactly like I told him."

There are so many stories about the Derby that no one can tell them all. Two fellows who know as many as anyone and can tell them better than most wrote the book you're reading now. I've known Joe Hirsch of the *Daily Racing Form* for more than thirty years, both as a friend and as a writer, and he is closer to the Derby scene than anybody. Jim Bolus, who for many years was the racing editor of the *Louisville Times*, has devoted much of his life to writing about the Derby and the people who participate in it.

Kentucky Derby captures the flavor and spirit of Derby Day, with its stories about the heroes and the stars of yesterday and today, and its superb color photography, which brings the Derby right into your home. It's a great book, both for professionals as well as for those who have never bet a quarter on a horse. The Kentucky Derby is an institution, uniquely American and as lively as a brass band, and here it all is, between two covers.

I hope you enjoy it as much as I did. It certainly helped me to relive some wonderful memories.

Eddie Arcaro

When I was approached to write this book, I invited the participation of the Kentucky Derby's most devoted historian, Jim Bolus of Louisville. Jim has been particularly close to the Derby scene for years, as racing editor of the *Louisville Times* and as the author of *Run for the Roses*. It has been a happy collaboration with an old friend.

For those of you who know the Kentucky Derby and love it as we do, and for those of you who know little more than what is seen on television on the first Saturday in May, we hope that we have added to your knowledge and understanding of the ways and heroes of the Derby, and to your enjoyment of it, too.

Joe Hirsch

Born to Run

**F**arm manager of Claiborne, John Sosby, says: "Most of the foals arrive at night. It's quiet and peaceful and the mares are relaxed, and before you know it they're down and the foals begin to pop out. You help the mares to deliver, and when you see the foals struggling to their feet you think to yourself, 'This is the one.' They fall and struggle back to their feet again and you look them over and say, 'Is this the one who'll get us a Kentucky Derby?' "

Claiborne Farm's Swale, a star-crossed colt who rocketed to the heavens and then faded from sight, was "the one" on Derby Day, 1984. A son of 1977 Kentucky Derby winner, Seattle Slew, he was foaled at 10:40 P.M. on April 21, 1981, at the farm in Paris, Kentucky.

The Kentucky Derby is for 3-year-olds, and any registered thoroughbred foal of 1981 was eligible for the 1984 Derby, if nominated by his stable. The 1984 Run for the Roses drew 312 nominees. Of these, some failed to measure up in prep races, others were injured along the way. Through the weeding-out process, the 1984 Derby attracted twenty starters, the maximum under rules adopted in the mid-1970s.

Making it to the Derby is a major accomplishment. In 1981 Swale, a colt, was one of 38,629 foals registered with the Jockey Club from the United States and Canada. Of these, approximately half were fillies. Only thirty-four fillies have run in the first 113 Kentucky Derbys and only two have won. So for practical purposes, Swale's chances were estimated to be 1 in 19,000.

Despite the odds, Sosby had high expectations. He thought, "The breeding is there. His Old Man won the Derby. He's a nicely-made foal, not perfect, but very nice, and he seems to have a nice disposition. So Woody will like him."

Woody is Woodford C. Stephens, the Hall of Fame trainer who for the past twenty years has had in his care some of the fine horses raised at Claiborne Farm. But Woody also trains for other stables, and he had a brilliant 2-year-old in 1983 named Devil's Bag for the Hickory Tree Stable of James P. Mills.

Devil's Bag was champion of his division that season, and while Swale did well as a 2-year-old with five victories in seven starts and earnings of almost $500,000, it was Devil's Bag who was winter book favorite for the Derby and the most celebrated young horse since Secretariat.

Things did not go well at all in the spring of 1984 for either Devil's Bag or his trainer. The colt was not running well, and Stephens developed pneumonia and was hospitalized. Swale maintained steady progress, won the Florida Derby, but then was upset at Keeneland on an off track.

Training by telephone from the hospital, Stephens was despondent but determined. He came to the conclusion, after X-ray photos revealed a hairline fracture in Devil's Bag's knee, that the colt should be retired and that Swale would have to carry his hopes in the Derby. With Stephens on hand, Swale took the lead early on, ran away from the field, and won comfortably by more than three lengths. He was The One.

Two weeks later at the Preakness, on a track he did not like, and fatigued after a demanding workout that Stephens supervised, Swale finished out of the money as a 4–5 favorite. Three weeks after that, fully recovered and in peak form, Swale ran away with the Belmont Stakes, winning by four lengths with Stephens by his side.

Eight days later, returning from the track after a gallop on a quiet Sunday morning, Swale was being bathed on a grassy patch outside the barn when he suddenly reared over backward, fell to the ground, and died before veterinary assistance could respond. While experts conducted a careful autopsy, they were not certain about the cause of death. They thought it was a heart attack, but Stephens knew no horse could do what Swale did and have a bad heart. He was all heart, and when they buried him at Claiborne Farm, John Sosby said to himself, "He was the one. We never had a chance to get a mare to him, and that's too bad, because he had to make a sire. But we had him, at least for a short time."

Claiborne at the Derby

Much of Kentucky Derby history has been made at Claiborne Farm. Through years of hard work, the Hancock family established this farm as one of the finest in the world. It is a tricky and unpredictable thing, this business of breeding racehorses, and when somebody would ask Arthur B. "Bull" Hancock, Jr., what his secret to breeding was, he was known to reply, "We just try to do the usual unusually well."

For three generations now, the Hancock family has done the usual so unusually well that it has put its stamp on Kentucky Derby winners time and time again.

Arthur B. Hancock, Sr., the man who started the family breeding operation, bred 1939 Derby winner Johnstown and was the co-breeder of Jet Pilot, the 1947 victor. His grandson, Arthur B. Hancock III, was the co-breeder of 1982 Derby winner Gato Del Sol, who was born at his Stone Farm, just down the road from Claiborne. And Claiborne bred Swale, the 1984 Derby champion.

Syndication Savvy

But there's more to the Hancocks' Derby contributions than their breeding of these four winners. This family has been instrumental in syndicating stallions who have left their marks on the Derby, in purchasing the right horse for their clients, and in boarding mares for some of racing's most influential people.

Nowadays syndicating horses is a common practice. Syndication spreads the risk involved with these valuable animals. Instead of wholly owning one stallion and relying too much on that horse's performance at the stud, a person can belong to a

number of syndicates, thereby diversifying his breeding operation and enhancing his opportunities for success. As a syndicate member, a person has breeding rights to that particular stallion.

Years ago, syndicates usually were divided into shares of thirty or thirty-two, and later thirty-six. With syndication prices skyrocketing, however, today the usual number of shares has been increased to forty in order to keep them affordable.

Through the years, the Hancocks have played a big role in the syndication of stallions. In 1925 Arthur B. Hancock, Sr., organized a four-man syndicate that paid $125,000 to bring Sir Gallahad III to this country from France. In 1936 he completed arrangements for the importation of the syndicated Blenheim II from England.

Sir Gallahad III sired a Triple Crown winner, Gallant Fox (1930), in his initial season at Claiborne, and so did Blenheim II, siring Triple Crown king Whirlaway (1941). Blenheim II also sired Jet Pilot, the 1947 Derby winner.

And then there was the syndication of Nasrullah. Bull Hancock, who took over the management of Claiborne in 1949, bought Nasrullah that year on behalf of a syndicate, and the 9-year-old stallion was brought to this country from Ireland. Nasrullah never did sire a Derby winner, but his blood flowed in later generations of Derby victors; he was the grandsire of two Derby winners and the great-grandsire of six others.

A Syndication Coup

When Bull Hancock's son Seth took over the management of Claiborne at the age of twenty-three, he scored a syndication coup of his own. C.T. Chenery, who founded the Meadow Stable and had raced such good horses as Hill Prince, Third Brother, Sir Gaylord, First Landing, and Cicada under Casey Hayes, died in 1973. His heirs, including his daughter, Helen "Penny" Chenery Tweedy, needed to pay huge inheritance taxes of $10 million on his vast estate to retain the racing stable.

Sir Gallahad III

At the time, Meadow Stable had two top colts: the 3-year-old 1972 Kentucky Derby and Belmont winner, Riva Ridge, and the 2-year-old Horse of the Year, Secretariat. As the director of the stable's operation, Mrs. Tweedy turned to young Hancock, who was able to syndicate Secretariat for a then-record $6,080,000, based on $190,000 per share for thirty-two shares. He also syndicated Riva Ridge for $5,120,000, or $160,000 a share for thirty-two shares.

Bull Hancock's Legacy

In 1972 Bull Hancock died, never having won the race that meant so much to him. "If there's one race I want to win, it's the Kentucky Derby," he had said. "For a hardboot like me, there's no race like the Derby."

Even though he failed to triumph in the Derby, his breeding efforts and expertise would show up in the pedigrees of five Derby winners during a six-year stretch in the 1980s.

First, there was Gato Del Sol, co-owned by Bull's eldest son, Arthur B. Hancock III. Gato Del Sol's dam, Peacefully, was sired by Jacinto, who was bred by Claiborne. Following the 1982 Derby, young Hancock remembered his father, saying, "This is the greatest thing that can happen to me in this life. I saw how much Daddy wanted to win the whole thing. I'd like to dedicate this trophy to my dad. He taught me everything I know—and how to get it."

Next came Sunny's Halo, the 1983 Derby winner. He was out of Mostly Sunny, who was sired by Sunny, a horse bred by Bull Hancock.

Then, in 1984, Bull's other son, Seth, the president of Claiborne, won the Derby with Swale. He also remembered his father after the victory, saying, "This Derby is a tribute to my father. This Derby is his Derby. He raced Swale's mother."

Indeed, Tuerta, the dam of Swale, was the last horse to win a stakes race for Claiborne while Bull Hancock was alive (the 1972 Blue Hen Stakes at Delaware Park).

In 1986 Mrs. Howard B. Keck's Derby winner, Ferdinand, traced his roots to Claiborne, having been foaled there, broken there, and sired by Nijinsky II, a stallion standing at the Paris, Kentucky, farm. Thirty years earlier—at a 1956 Keeneland sale—Bull Hancock made a successful bid of $72,000 to acquire Vulcania, an 8-year-old mare, on behalf of Howard Keck. Vulcania turned out to be a great-granddam of Ferdinand. Flaring Top, Ferdinand's great-granddam on his sire's side, had been bred by none other than A.B. Hancock, Sr.

And in 1987, Derby winner Alysheba was out of Bel Sheba, a daughter of Lt. Stevens, who was bred by Claiborne.

Among the people for whom the Hancocks have boarded mares are the Kecks, William Woodward, Sr., and the Phipps family. Woodward, the Belair Stud owner, kept most of his breeding stock at Claiborne, and his two Triple Crown champions—Gallant Fox and Omaha—both were born there. Bold Ruler, a Nasrullah colt who raced for the Wheatley Stable of Mrs. Henry Carnegie Phipps, also was foaled at Claiborne. As a matter of fact, Bold Ruler and Round Table were foaled on the same day (April 6, 1954) at Claiborne, and they were destined to win acclaim as Horse of the Year in 1957 and 1958, respectively.

Bold Ruler and Round Table both ran in the '57 Derby, which produced the greatest field in the race's history. Round Table finished third and Bold Ruler fourth in the race won by Calumet Farm's Iron Liege.

A Derby Dynasty

Calumet has bred and raced a record eight Derby winners, five of whom were descendants of Bull Lea, an also-ran in the 1938 Derby. In its immaculate horse cemetery, Calumet has markers for its many star racehorses and famous broodmares. The biggest marker of all—a bronze statue—is over the grave of Bull Lea.

Calumet has not run many also-rans in the Derby,

Bull Lea

E.P. Taylor at 1974 Queen's Plate

Steve Penrod, Renee Lickle, William Lickle, Keith Allen, Seth Hancock, and Queen Elizabeth II in 1985

Samuel Riddle, left

Mrs. Penny Chenery Tweedy and Gerard J. McKeon

Colonel E.R. Bradley in 1940

Arthur B. "Bull" Hancock, Jr., Harris Robinson,
Arthur B. Hancock, Sr.

Warren Wright

Mrs. Gene Markey

but it took some time—ten years—before the farm walked away with the roses at Churchill Downs. In 1931, three years after his family sold its interest in the Calumet Baking Powder Company for a reported $40 million, Warren Wright, Sr., converted Calumet Farm from a standardbred to a thoroughbred nursery when he inherited the Lexington, Kentucky, establishment from his father, William M. Wright.

Wright spent large sums of money to acquire the finest in bloodstock, and in 1936 he made the soundest investment of his life by purchasing Bull Lea for $14,000 at a Saratoga yearling auction. The colt ran a mediocre eighth in the 1938 Derby but finished his career the next year with earnings of $94,825, an outstanding return on his purchase price. But his real value was to come at stud, where he served as the backbone of the farm's breeding operation, turning Calumet into a racing dynasty in the 1940s and 1950s. Calumet won its first Derby in 1941 with Whirlaway, who went on to provide the farm with its first Triple Crown sweep. Seven years later, Citation also won the Triple Crown for Calumet. Citation was one of three Derby winners sired by Bull Lea, the other two being Hill Gail (1952) and Iron Liege (1957).

Bradley's Bargain

Just as Bull Lea turned out to be a tremendous bargain for Wright, a horse named Black Toney rewarded Colonel E.R. Bradley many times over at stud. When Bradley, a lifelong gambler and sportsman, paid $1,600 for Black Toney as a yearling in 1912, he acquired a horse who would prove to be highly influential in his breeding operation.

Bradley, the master of Idle Hour Stock Farm near Lexington, owned four Derby winners, breeding three of them himself—Behave Yourself (1921), Bubbling Over (1926), and Brokers Tip (1933). Bradley bred his other Derby winner, Burgoo King (1932), a son of Bubbling Over, in partnership with Horace Davis.

Triple Crown Races

Black Toney sired forty stakes winners, including two Derby victors—Brokers Tip and Black Gold, the latter triumphing in 1924 for Mrs. Rosa Hoots of Oklahoma.

Bimelech, the best colt ever sired by Black Toney, went off as a heavy favorite in the 1940 Derby but ran second for Bradley. Blue Larkspur, the favorite in the '29 Derby, also failed for Bradley, coming in fourth. Had Bradley captured the Derby as he figured to with Blue Larkspur and Bimelech, he would have surpassed the breeders' record at that time of five Derby winners—held by John E. Madden of Hamburg Place.

The Wizard of the Turf

Appropriately known as "The Wizard of the Turf," Madden was perhaps the best all-around horseman in the sport's history. He bred horses and then trained them and then sold them. "Better to sell and repent than keep and repent," he said. His Derby winners were Old Rosebud (1914), Sir Barton (1919), Paul Jones (1920), Zev (1923), and Flying Ebony (1925).

Birthdays

A horse's foaling date can have a bearing on his maturity, which may affect the price he brings at auction. The official birthday—not the actual birth date—for all thoroughbreds born each year in the Northern Hemisphere is January 1. In the Southern Hemisphere, it is July 1.

Most Derby winners have been foaled in March or April. Lawrin, the 1938 victor, was an especially early foal, having been born on January 30, 1935. And then there are certain Derby winners who were not actually 3 years old at the time they ran for the roses. Northern Dancer, who triumphed in 1964, was foaled on May 27, 1961.

Canadian-Bred Northern Dancer

Northern Dancer's breeding was a bit of a coincidence. In 1960 his dam, Natalma, a daughter of Native Dancer, had been training brilliantly for

Year	Horse	Jockey	Owner	Trainer
1919	Sir Barton	John Loftus	J.K.L. Ross	H.G. Bedwell
1930	Gallant Fox	Earl Sande	Belair Stud	James Fitzsimmons
1935	Omaha	William Saunders	Belair Stud	James Fitzsimmons
1937	War Admiral	Charles Kurtsinger	Samuel D. Riddle	George Conway
1941	Whirlaway	Eddie Arcaro	Calumet Farm	Ben A. Jones
1943	Count Fleet	John Longden	Mrs. J.D. Hertz	Don Cameron
1946	Assault	Warren Mehrtens	King Ranch	Max Hirsch
1948	Citation	Eddie Arcaro	Calumet Farm	Ben A. Jones
1973	Secretariat	Ron Turcotte	C.T. Chenery	Lucien Laurin
1977	Seattle Slew	Jean Cruguet	Karen L. Taylor	William Turner, Jr.
1978	Affirmed	Steve Cauthen	Harbor View Farm	Lazaro S. Barrera

the Kentucky Oaks when she fractured her knee. "We were undecided what to do," recalled Joe Thomas, the late vice-president of thoroughbred operations at Windfields Farm. "It was a question of whether we were going to do surgery on her and bring her back or breed her. We had had another filly by Native Dancer the previous year that had come up with the same problem. We had done surgery on her, but it hadn't worked.

"So we just kicked it around and said, 'Oh, what the hell, why don't we breed her to Nearctic and if she gets in foal, okay; if she doesn't get in foal, then maybe we'll do the surgery and try to bring her back.' So by the time we got her back to Canada and got her bred, it was almost the end of June."

Natalma was the last mare bred to Nearctic that year. With the eleven-month gestation period, Northern Dancer wasn't born until May 27, making him a very late foal.

As a yearling he was offered for sale for $25,000, but there were no takers, so his breeder, E.P. Taylor, kept the little fellow.

Northern Dancer was proof that top racehorses can come in small packages. When he ran in the Derby, he was a hand shorter than Hill Rise, the favorite. Second choice in the wagering, Northern Dancer won the Derby in track-record time of 2:00 under Bill Hartack, holding off a late surge by Hill Rise. Afterward, Jim Murray of the *Los Angeles Times* wrote: "Northern Dancer is the kind of a colt who, if you saw him in your living room, you'd send for a trap and put cheese in it. He's so little, a cat would chase him. But he's so plucky, there's barely room in him for his heart. His legs are barely long enough to keep his tail off the ground. He probably takes a hundred more strides than anyone else in the race, but he's harder to pass than a third martini."

Northern Dancer went on to win the Preakness, too, but he was unable to stay the Belmont's mile-and-a-half, finishing third.

The fact that Northern Dancer could accelerate carried him a long way. As Thomas put it, "In the Derby, he was sitting in there and when the hole opened up, Hartack said go. He just stepped on it, and he was gone. That faculty is what made Northern Dancer go a lot farther than people thought that he should. Many considered him to be basically a miler. But he had the ability to accelerate, and you could rate him."

Snow and Ice

E.P. Taylor, the Canadian who bred and raced Northern Dancer, received plenty of advice from folks who bred horses in Kentucky. Some was good. Some was not.

Certain hardboots told Taylor, "What have you got up there in Canada? Snow and ice. There's no way you can breed a good horse there."

All Taylor did was to breed such champions as Northern Dancer, English Triple Crown winner Nijinsky II, Epsom Derby winner The Minstrel, and many other outstanding horses.

Northern Dancer has proven to be the most successful commercial stallion in history. Through 1986, he had sired a record 123 stakes winners, including twenty-three champions. Quite an accomplishment for a horse who could have been purchased for $25,000 as a yearling.

Northern Dancer stood in Canada for his first four seasons (1965–1968). He was getting some pretty good mares, but there was a certain amount of resistance to sending good mares to Canada. In December 1968, he was moved to Windfields Farm in Maryland.

Growing Pains

In contrast to the smallish Northern Dancer, 1935 Derby and Triple Crown winner Omaha was a big horse. He was foaled at Claiborne Farm on March 24, 1932, the same day of the month that such other well-known horses as 1934 Kentucky Derby winner Cavalcade and 1943 Triple Crown champion Count Fleet were born.

Omaha developed into an impressive, long-bodied colt who was to stand 16.2 hands (66 inches from his withers to the ground) during the prime of his racing career. He was so large that he required double-room accommodations at the racetrack. "Everywhere we went with him, they'd have to give him two stalls," recalled William "Smokey" Saunders, the jockey who rode Omaha in his Triple Crown sweep. "They'd take two stalls and knock the partition out in the middle to make one huge stall."

Retirement Days

Few Derby winners race beyond their 4-year-old seasons anymore. Some are retired prematurely due to injuries; others have been hurried off to the breeding shed for lucrative careers at stud. Most Derby winners come back to Kentucky to stand in the Bluegrass area. Secretariat and Spectacular Bid are at Claiborne, Seattle Slew is at Three Chimneys Farm, and Affirmed is at Calumet.

When Secretariat finished his career and came to Kentucky to be retired in the fall of 1973, approximately 100 newsmen and spectators were on hand to greet him at Lexington's Blue Grass Field. As the four-engine plane carrying him approached the airport, pilot Neff Dee received the following message from the tower: "There are more people here to meet Secretariat than there are when the governor comes in."

Recalling the tower's message, Dee later said with a laugh, "We told them that Secretariat won more races than the governor."

Secretariat took up residence at Claiborne in the same stall that had housed his father, Bold Ruler, who died in 1971. The first Triple Crown winner in a quarter of a century and the toast of the racing world in 1973, Secretariat has remained popular in retirement. Those who visit Claiborne Farm inevitably want to see the big red horse.

Modern-day Derby winners enjoy the life of Riley, servicing a book of mares each year and grazing in peaceful surroundings. But not *all* Derby winners have had it so good. Typhoon II, who won the 1897 Derby, was pulling a milk wagon in 1911.

Times do change.

We love horses without wondering why. We just do. The horse is everything we would like this world to be— strong and beautiful, perfect in creation.

Come with us to the farm in the morning. Take the two-lane asphalt. Leave the city behind. The land invites you out.

This land is pasture, soft rolling hills, pillowy clouds of bluegrass. Black fences reach across the lush green. And horses move in silent beauty. They raise their heads to listen. They look to the horizon. They have come millions of years to this moment.

There is dew on the pasture grass. At the farm, the first light of morning transforms the dew into diamonds.

We see a dream.

*Oft
not
cho
in i
to s
abo
Sai
"Ne
sur*

Slew

Bold

Schooling Winners

The yearling enters the sales ring, whinnying as he is led into the arena by a stud groom. He is a bright-looking yearling, this handsome chestnut with a distinct blaze and one white stocking. His conformation is nearly perfect, and he has a pedigree laced with champions for several generations. But will he prove to be a runner?

They have come from all over to inspect the horses at Keeneland's prestigious, high-powered July Selected Yearling Sale. And this particular yearling is the one that those with the deepest pockets want to see. For several days the prospective buyers have been by his barn in the Keeneland stable area, checking him closely: watching him walk to make sure that he moves flawlessly; feeling his legs; looking at his head, his shoulder, his ankles.

The yearling has no name at this stage of his life. As is the custom at these sales, he wears a hip number as a means of identification. Now that he has stepped into the ring, the bidding will soon commence. The interested buyers sit back in theater-type seats and enjoy the air-conditioning.

Woodburn Sales

Horse sales have not always provided such comfort. Take those held at the Woodburn Farm of A.J. Alexander, the Derby's most successful breeder of the nineteenth century. Alexander bred four Derby winners—Baden-Baden (1877), Fonso (1880), Joe Cotton (1885), and Chant (1894)—at his Kentucky farm.

The yearling sales at Woodburn frequently drew some of the most famous horsemen in the country, men like August Belmont I and James R. Keene and the Dwyer Brothers. Yet these were by no means fancy sales. Unlike today, when yearlings are groomed to look their very best for buyers, the Woodburn youngsters were allowed to run loose until the time of the sale. The Woodburn people would remove any burrs, but that was about the extent of the sales preparation. Not only that, the bidders sat right down on the ground, or they stood under trees. Quite a contrast from today.

But the object of the buyers was the same then as it is now: to pick out that yearling who will go on to provide the chance of a lifetime.

First Time Lucky

Fred W. Hooper was looking for just such a horse in 1943, the year that Keeneland held its first yearling sale. This auction took place under a tent in the paddock. In looking around at the sale, Hooper spotted Hip No. 134, a yearling sired by Sir Gallahad III. The colt was a bay with a few white hairs on his forehead.

"He just caught my eye, the way he walked and all," Hooper recalled. "Didn't have a lot of flesh on him. He just looked real smart. So I bought him for $10,200."

This particular yearling, named Hoop Jr., was the first thoroughbred ever purchased by Hooper. The colt ran in the 1945 Derby, and before the race Hooper expressed just how important it was to him. "I'd rather win the Kentucky Derby than make a million dollars in my construction business," he said.

Hoop Jr. took an early lead in the Derby and stayed in front all the way, hitting the finish line six lengths on top. "I never thought I'd make it this quick," Hooper said afterward.

Hoop Jr. came from a good family, being a son of Sir Gallahad III, who had sired two previous Derby winners—Gallant Fox (1930) and Gallahadion (1940). In addition, One Hour, the dam of Hoop Jr., was a stakes-winning racemare who had produced three stakes winners.

Record Book Sales

Now, as then, buyers at sales have two major factors to consider when they shop for yearlings—

a horse's pedigree and conformation. The sales announcer mentions the most important points in the yearling's pedigree, and once he is finished, the auctioneer asks for an opening bid.

In 1973 legendary auctioneer George Swinebroad was astonished when he heard the opening bid on a son of Bold Ruler at the Keeneland summer sale. Slamming his gavel down, the auctioneer said, "Well, that's a nice opener, I'll say that—best we've had in a long time. I've got $500,000 as an opening bid!"

The all-time high price for a yearling is now $13.1 million, a record that was set in 1985 at Keeneland. But in 1973, the world record was $510,000. So a bid of $500,000 would get a person's attention in those days—and yet it held up for only seven seconds. That is how long it took Jim Scully, a Lexington bloodstock agent who had formed a syndicate, to make the next and final bid of $600,000. This two-bid sale set a world record in a dramatic yearling auction.

The yearling, consigned by Claiborne Farm, turned out to be worth the price. Named Wajima, he missed the Triple Crown series in 1975 because of injury but was voted the champion 3-year-old colt of that season. When he was syndicated for stud duty at Spendthrift Farm in 1975, his price of $7.2 million also set a record.

Behind the Scenes

Bidding at sales usually involves quite a few more raises than the sale of Wajima in 1973. Bidding generally is done subtly, a raised finger here, an almost imperceptible nod there. Bid spotters are trained to look for these signs. Moments after the auction opens, an electronic display board in the Keeneland pavilion lights up the bids and keeps track of the price, which goes onward and upward.

The bidding is sometimes conducted behind the scenes. In 1983 at Keeneland, certain bids came from within the pavilion, but the real war took place in the holding area behind the pavilion. The two rival bidders were separated by a partition. On one side, bidding for a syndicate that included Robert Sangster, was Joss Collins. On the other side was Colonel Dick Warden, a bloodstock adviser for Sheik Mohammed bin Rashid al Maktoum. Warden won out in the bidding duel, going to $10.2 million, but the yearling, named Snaafi Dancer, wound up plagued with more than his share of bad luck. He never started at the races, and when he was sent to the stud, he was discovered to have a fertility problem although he showed signs of improvement in 1987.

A Bargain Bid

Whatever the price a yearling brings, only time will answer that one all-important question of how he runs.

Despite good looks and impeccable breeding, there is no assurance at this stage of a yearling's life that he has what it takes to make a name for himself at the races. The yearling sales business quite obviously is a gamble, a high-risk game played for big stakes.

And Keeneland is the place where buyers come prepared to spend the biggest money. Millions of dollars are paid out there each summer as people from all over the globe converge on the Lexington, Kentucky, sales facility to acquire the finest in horseflesh.

But there are other sales that produce champion runners and Derby winners, including the Saratoga Yearling Sales in August, Fasig-Tipton's Kentucky Summer Yearling Sale, and another Keeneland yearling sale in September. Spectacular Bid, the 1979 Derby winner, came from the 1977 September sale at Keeneland. Although his breeders had tried to enter him in Keeneland's summer sale, he had not measured up to the necessary standards because the breeding on his dam's side was considered weak.

Spectacular Bid thus was relegated to the September sale and was one of 1,425 yearlings who went through the ring at the five-day vendue. "We

1. Forehead
2. Neck
3. Withers
4. Back
5. Loins
6. Hip joint
7. Quarter
8. Cannon
9. Stifle
10. Flank
11. Ribs
12. Pastern
13. Hoof
14. Fetlock joint (ankle)
15. Knee
16. Forearm
17. Point of shoulder

liked him an awful lot," said Grover "Bud" Delp, who trained the colt for Hawksworth Farm, owned by Harry, Teresa, and Tom Meyerhoff. "I think they were prepared to go up to sixty grand for him."

As it was, Spectacular Bid sold for $37,000, which proved to be one of the greatest bargains in the sport's history. In 1980 he was syndicated for $22 million and retired to Claiborne Farm with earnings of $2,781,608, both record figures at the time.

Importance of Conformation

Nobody knows for sure how good a horse is until after a few starts. You can imagine then how difficult it must be to try to look at a yearling and determine whether or not he will prove to be a runner.

Derby winners have come in all shapes and sizes—big and little, tall and short. But when a horseman looks for a particular type of horse—when he is checking out conformation at a sale, for instance—he does have certain things in mind.

"A big thing is to recognize balance," said Bill Clark, a veteran horseman from Midway, Kentucky. "Balance comes with how they're put together. Balance causes a horse's racing motion to be fluid. A fluid motion helps him stay sound, in my opinion. A little, short, choppy horse that digs in real fast, that's not a good fluid motion. But a horse that's balanced has a very even stride, hits the ground in pretty good shape and all that."

"I'm great on soundness," Clark added. "I don't care how much ability a horse has, you have to be able to get him to the races. Also, I do like a good, big eye on a horse. That does a lot for me."

The inner qualities of a horse are all-important, sometimes making up for physical shortcomings. "Heart, that takes care of everything, but you can't look at it," Clark said with a chuckle. "Listen, I could break up racing if I could look at that heart."

Recalling his purchase of the 1960 Derby winner, Venetian Way, at Keeneland's 1958 summer sale,

Clark said, "He had no faults that I could find. He didn't bring but $10,500, so there were a whole lot of people who didn't like him."

Horses are competing in races, not beauty contests, so looks sometimes can be deceiving. A case in point was Broadway Limited, who ran in the 1930 Derby. In 1928 W.T. Waggoner, a cattle baron and oil man from Texas, and his trainer, C.E. "Boots" Durnell, bought Broadway Limited, a son of Man o' War, at the Saratoga yearling sale. This yearling had the breeding, and he had the looks. To buy him, Waggoner had to go to $65,000, which tied for third among the highest prices paid in America and abroad for yearlings in 1928. In nine starts the star-crossed Broadway Limited never finished in the money, never earned a penny. He finished far back in the 1930 Derby.

The stable gelded Broadway Limited during the summer of his 3-year-old season. He ran only once as a gelding, and in that race just two years after he had created such a stir at the Saratoga yearling sale, he dropped dead, a victim of heart failure.

Horses do not have to have perfect conformation to be top runners. "Horses run with all kinds of defects in their conformation," Clark said. "I won't spend a lot of money to buy a horse with a defect. A lot of them will stay sound, but a lot of them won't."

Choosing a Winner

A horse's conformation and pedigree can fool people, and the sales sometimes produce rags-to-riches stories. Canonero II, the 1971 Derby and Preakness winner, was a colt with a crooked right foreleg and an unimpressive pedigree. He was purchased by agent Luis Navas at Keeneland's 1969 September sale for $1,200, the lowest price of any Kentucky Derby winner ever sold at Keeneland.

"Canonero had an absolutely blank pedigree," Keeneland's former director of sales, William S. Evans, recalled. "His poor pedigree as well as his conformation pointed to his $1,200 selling price. This was 'catching lightning in a bottle.'"

Wide face and chest, toes in   *Lop ears, narrow chest, toes out*

Elementary Lessons

After a colt is purchased, he is taken to a farm, such as Claiborne, to begin schooling. Yearlings that are not sold but remain at their birthplace similarly enter a training regimen. Swale, the 1984 Kentucky Derby winner, learned his early lessons at Claiborne. He was broken there, just as many other top horses have been over the years, horses like 1986 Derby winner Ferdinand, as well as Round Table, Bold Ruler, Ruffian, Moccasin, Vitriolic, Chief's Crown, Misty Morn, and Dike.

Breaking usually begins in July or August of a horse's yearling year and lasts 50 to 120 days. Breaking a horse means introducing him to such equipment as the saddle and bridle, and to the feeling of weight on his back. He also learns what it is like to gallop on a racetrack. "We're trying to teach him the proper, basic training that he will need to carry with him throughout his life as a racehorse," Claiborne's John Sosby said.

At Claiborne the breaking of a yearling typically begins in a stall with an exercise boy or girl "bellying" the horse—that is, lying across the horse's back. "We will keep them in the stall for ten to twelve days," Sosby said. "We'll figure-eight; we'll get off, we'll get on; we'll get him used to rubbing on him; we'll get him used to the rider's feet where they're moving them up on his shoulder and back on his flanks. We'll really work with him so he'll understand that this is what it's all about."

Breaking a yearling is a step-by-step process. According to Sosby, "You've got to give them plenty of time—all the time in the world—because they're young, and you're trying to teach them the right things. They'll learn enough bad habits without you teaching them any."

Those yearlings leaving Claiborne are also familiarized with a starting gate. "We'll walk them through the starting gate," Sosby said. "We'll never fasten them in, and we'll never break them out of the gate. We leave that up to the trainer to teach them the way he wants them to break from the gate. I figure that at the end of ninety days, these horses are ready to go anywhere."

When it comes to breaking yearlings, Bob Moore is another person who speaks as an authority with many years of experience. Now retired, Moore was associated with the breaking of five Kentucky Derby winners (Citation, Hill Gail, Iron Liege, Tim Tam, and Proud Clarion) and one winner of the Epsom Derby (Roberto).

"To properly break a thoroughbred and to teach him the fundamentals of the racetrack isn't something that you do overnight," Moore said. "It takes four months to teach the basics. Now that's not getting him fit to breeze or work or anything like that. At the end of four months, you might have him up to galloping about a mile—at a normal gallop, not a fast gallop, because you can't go very fast with these young horses. If you do, you'll upset their joints."

Moore recalls that Citation was an easy horse to break. "He was very sensible, a great mover," he said. "I knew he was a good horse. But I didn't know he was as good as he was. Even Ben Jones didn't know that until he got to running him."

Trainers' Secrets

Trainers who instruct horses after their initial schooling have to know their students to get the most out of them. "Sunny Jim" Fitzsimmons trained three Kentucky Derby winners—Gallant Fox (1930), Omaha (1935), and Johnstown (1939)—and he knew how to obtain the best results from his runners.

Of Gallant Fox, Fitzsimmons said, "So long as he had competition he would run like the wind, but as soon as he whipped everybody and got the lead, he would slow to a walk. He was a fire-eater when he had the competition, though."

Fitzsimmons saw to it that Gallant Fox had the competition in his workouts. The crafty trainer was known to use a relay team of horses at work. A sprint horse would start off with Gallant Fox, and at some point along the way, another would step in and pick up the action. Sometimes still another trial

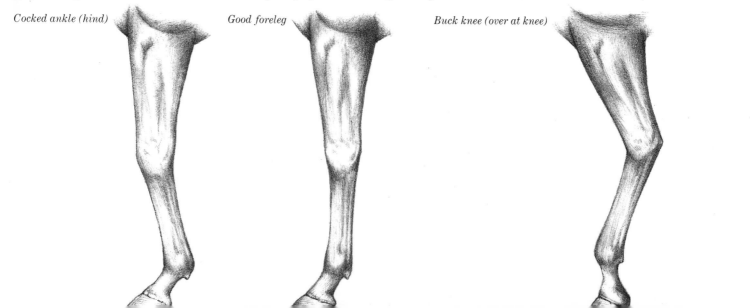

Cocked ankle (hind)   *Good foreleg*   *Buck knee (over at knee)*

horse would come in as a replacement and hook Gallant Fox. All the better to keep the Fox running hard throughout the workout.

Sometimes to get the best results from a horse, his stable must keep the opposition in the dark. Take the case of Omaha. William 'Smokey' Saunders, who began riding Omaha in his 3-year-old season in 1935, recalled that the colt would "savage" a horse that bumped or brushed him. That is, Omaha would try to take a bite out of a horse that got too close. Saunders said that Omaha's savaging propensity was a very well-kept secret. "I think that the exercise boy, myself, and Mr. Fitzsimmons were the only ones that knew about it."

As a juvenile, Omaha earned a meager $3,850, the lowest 2-year-old earnings for any Triple Crown winner in history. But his best would be yet to come. Gallant Fox, his sire, had turned into a champion after his 2-year-old season, and so it would be with Omaha.

Prep Races

Two-year-old champions have had different degrees of success in the Kentucky Derby. During the 1970s, six of them (Riva Ridge, Secretariat, Foolish Pleasure, Seattle Slew, Affirmed, and Spectacular Bid) won the Derby. But during the 1980s, not a single juvenile champion has triumphed in the Derby.

The number of starts for a 2-year-old varies. Donau, the 1910 Derby winner, hardly had time to catch his breath as a 2-year-old, racing all of forty-one times in 1909. At the other extreme was Apollo, the only Derby winner (1882) who did not even compete at 2. Three other Derby winners—Leonatus (1883), Tim Tam (1958), and Lucky Debonair (1965)—started only once as juveniles.

After a horse turns 3, the number of prep races that he has leading up to the Derby also varies. As strange as it may seem now, certain horses in the old days made the first start of their 3-year-old campaigns in the Derby. With fewer opportunities to run in prep races in those days, horsemen sometimes trained their 3-year-olds up to the Derby, and workouts of a mile and a quarter were not uncommon.

Among those whose 3-year-old debuts came in the Derby were Baden-Baden, Riley, Ben Brush, Plaudit, Lieut. Gibson, His Eminence, Alan-a-Dale, Sir Huon, Regret, Exterminator, Sir Barton, and Morvich, all winners of the big race. The filly Regret ran in just three races as a 2-year-old, all at six furlongs and all in August. So when she entered the Derby, she had only sprinted in her races, and she had not competed for more than eight months. Nowadays, a trainer would be ridiculed if he dared to run a horse into the Derby off such past performances. But nobody was laughing at Regret's trainer, Jimmy Rowe, Sr., in 1915. Especially after she defeated her fifteen male opponents.

A trainer needs to give his Derby candidate the proper foundation while guarding against doing too much with the horse. It is a fine line, and the Derby is no place for amateur horsemen. In 1983 Sunny's Halo became the first Derby winner since Jet Pilot in 1947 to capture the classic after only two prep races as a 3-year-old. When trainer Lucien Laurin brought Riva Ridge into the Derby off just three prep races in 1972, he was criticized in certain corners for not having done enough with his horse. Laurin, however, knew his horse, and Riva Ridge won the Derby by 3¾ lengths. The next year, Laurin prepared Triple Crown winner Secretariat in the same way, racing him just three times at 3 before the Derby.

Some trainers, on the other hand, may have mishandled their horses leading up to the Derby. In 1940 Bimelech was hailed as a wonder horse, but finished second to long shot Gallahadion in the Derby. Bill Hurley, the trainer of Bimelech, was faulted by some observers for having let the colt go almost six months without a start and then running him in two prep races in less than a week's time. Almost without exception, the Derby is the first time that a horse has raced a mile and a quarter. The farthest distance most of the starters have tried

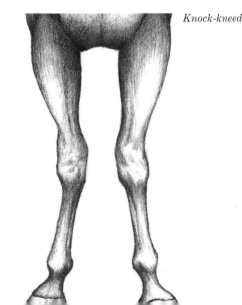

Knock-kneed

Date	Graded Stakes Races	Length	Track
Jan.	Tropical Park Derby	9f	Calder
Feb.	El Camino Real Derby	8.5f	Bay Meadows
Feb.	Everglades	9f	Hialeah
Feb.	San Vicente	7f	Santa Anita
Feb.	Flamingo*	9f	Hialeah
Mar.	San Rafael	8f	Santa Anita
Mar.	Swift	6f	Aqueduct
Mar.	Hutcheson	7f	Gulfstream
Mar.	Tampa Bay Derby	8.5f	Tampa Bay
Mar.	Louisiana Derby	9f	Fair Grounds
Mar.	Bay Shore	7f	Aqueduct
Mar.	San Felipe*	8.5f	Santa Anita
Mar.	Fountain of Youth	8.5f	Gulfstream
Mar.	Jim Beam	8.5f	Turfway
Apr.	Florida Derby*	9f	Gulfstream
Apr.	Santa Anita Derby*	9f	Santa Anita
Apr.	Gotham	8f	Aqueduct
Apr.	Lexington	8.5f	Keeneland
Apr.	Wood Memorial*	9f	Aqueduct
Apr.	Arkansas Derby*	9f	Oaklawn
Apr.	Garden State	9f	Garden State
Apr.	California Derby	9f	Golden State
Apr.	Blue Grass*	9f	Keeneland
Apr.	Derby Trial	8f	Churchill Downs

In preparation for the Derby, 3-year-olds are often entered in several of the Graded Stakes races listed above. Distances are given in furlongs (one furlong is one-eighth of a mile); the Kentucky Derby is 10 furlongs.

* Grade 1 races

coming into the Derby is a mile and an eighth. So the Derby answers the question that is ever present on the first Saturday in May—which horses can go a mile and a quarter and which cannot?

Three-Year-Old Trials

The roads that lead to Kentucky in the spring of the year may vary greatly. With New York traditionally attracting many of the best stables in the country, it is not surprising that more Triple Crown winners—six—have run in the Wood Memorial than in any other prep race. Gallant Fox (1930), Count Fleet (1943), Assault (1946), and Seattle Slew (1977) won the Wood. Omaha (1935) was a strong contender, and Secretariat finished third.

The Florida Derby also has had plenty of outstanding horses over the years. From its inception at Gulfstream Park in 1952 through 1987, the Florida Derby has sent runners on to rack up fourteen victories in the Kentucky Derby, as well as fifteen in the Preakness and ten in the Belmont.

Keeneland Race Course, located near Lexington, Kentucky, is another track that has served as a good proving ground for Derby candidates. Altogether, twenty Derby winners have run at Keeneland in the spring of their 3-year-old seasons, including fourteen who prepped in the Blue Grass Stakes. In 1959 Tomy Lee won the Blue Grass, and his trainer, Frank Childs, was outspoken in his praise of Keeneland, saying, "As far as I am concerned, there is no place in the world a horse blossoms more in spring than right here in the Blue Grass."

Tomy Lee went on to win the Derby, becoming the first Blue Grass product to do so since Shut Out in 1942. The Blue Grass, which had gone so long without sending a horse into the Derby's winner's circle, soon became *the* prep race to watch. For four straight years it turned out Derby winners— Decidedly (1962), Chateaugay (1963), Northern Dancer (1964), and Lucky Debonair (1965). After a

The Preakness

The Kentucky Derby

one-year lapse, two more Blue Grass starters wound up with the Derby's first-place check—Proud Clarion (1967) and Forward Pass (1968). Henry Forrest, the trainer of Forward Pass, said at Keeneland that year, "I believe horses do better here in the spring of the year. The Blue Grass is a good distance and at the right time on the schedule, if you have a horse good enough to win the Derby." Forrest added, "Of course, if you haven't got a good horse, it wouldn't make any difference if you got him ready for the Derby at Podunk."

The Blue Grass continued its successful record with Dust Commander (1970) and Riva Ridge (1972) triumphing in the Derby. Thus, nine Blue Grass starters in fourteen years picked up the Derby's top money. And then, over the next fourteen years, only two Blue Grass horses won the Derby— Spectacular Bid in 1979 and Gato Del Sol in 1982.

It is funny how trends change, how something that was once so popular can fall out of favor. While the Blue Grass was having its streak of success as a Derby prep race, horsemen marveled about the beneficial aspects of this prep and talked about the "magic" of the race. It was run at the right time (nine days before the Derby) and at the right distance (a mile and an eighth). But after the race produced only two Derby winners from 1973 through 1986, some horsemen said that it was run too close to the Derby. There was talk that maybe a change was in order for the Blue Grass, which was facing increased competition from other tracks in drawing top horses. Then along came 1987 Derby winner Alysheba, who finished first in the Blue Grass (although later he was disqualified and placed third for interference).

For years, few bettors at Churchill Downs paid attention to the Arkansas Derby winner. After all, the Arkansas Derby, founded in 1936, went forty-seven years without sending a winner on to capture the Kentucky Derby. Sunny's Halo finally ended that dry spell in 1983. Helped in recent years by a richer purse, the Arkansas Derby has been drawing better horses. Two Kentucky Derby favorites— Althea (1984) and Demons Begone (1987)—were Arkansas Derby winners. The mile-and-an-eighth race at Oaklawn Park also produced two Preakness winners since 1983—Gate Dancer (1984) and Tank's Prospect (1985).

Casualty List

The trail to the Derby frequently is strewn with horses who are injured along the way. In 1982, an internal blockage sidelined Derby favorite Timely Writer less than two weeks before the race, and then during Derby Week the highly regarded Hostage broke down in a workout.

The 1966 Derby was another that lost some genuine stars. Buckpasser was forced out of the entire Triple Crown series with a quarter crack, and Graustark fractured a foot in the Blue Grass, never to race again. In addition, Buffle was sent to Louisville but developed a fever and did not run in the Derby.

Pitfalls are ever present, even up to Derby Day itself. Calumet Farm's Gen. Duke was scratched from the 1957 renewal the morning of the race, and in 1931 Equipoise was entered in the Derby but was scratched just hours before post time due to a foot injury. Sir Gaylord was withdrawn from the '62 renewal on Derby Eve after fracturing a sesamoid in a half-mile blowout.

The list of casualties on the road to the Derby goes on and on: Stagehand in 1938, Burning Blaze in 1932, Carlaris in 1926, Grey Lag in 1921, Waldo in 1910, Dr. Leggo in 1905, and The Picket in 1903. There have been many others.

Besides injuries, the nomination list is further cut down by many candidates who simply do not run well enough in their prep race. That is not to say, however, that the preps always separate the contenders from the pretenders. Derby fever consumes many owners in the weeks leading up to the big race, and sometimes horses whose credentials do not seem to justify a starting spot in the big race wind up being entered anyway.

The Belmont

Triple Crown Nominations

Horses are entered in the Derby two days before the race at a fee of $10,000. To start in the race costs an additional $10,000.

Earlier in the year horses are nominated to the Derby. Actually, they are nominated to all three races in the Triple Crown series—the Derby, the Preakness, and the Belmont. In 1986 for the first time, Churchill Downs, Pimlico, and the New York Racing Association combined their nominating blanks for the Triple Crown.

An owner now has two opportunities to nominate to these three races. The first deadline, in mid-January, has a fee of $600 that covers all three events. Those who do not nominate at that time have one more chance, a final closing deadline in mid-March at a cost of $3,000 for the three races. If a horse is not nominated by then, he is not allowed to run in any Triple Crown event.

In 1987 bonus incentives were offered for the first time in the Triple Crown series, including a guaranteed $5 million total value to the winner of all three races, plus the purse money. Alysheba captured the Derby and the Preakness but finished fourth in the Belmont, missing out on the $5 million. He also missed out on a $1-million bonus offered to the owner of the horse with the best and most consistent finishes in the three races based on a point system. Had Alysheba finished second, he would have earned the $1 million. Instead, he came in fourth, slightly more than a neck behind second-place Cryptoclearance, and the bonus went to Belmont winner, Bet Twice, who had run second in both the Derby and the Preakness.

The Triple Crown carries great prestige and the winner of the Kentucky Derby almost always has gone on to the next leg of the series, the Preakness at Pimlico. Since 1934, there have been only two years—1982 and 1983—that failed to produce at least one horse who ran in all three Triple Crown races.

If you drive through Kentucky's heartland, over the soft hills that identify Louisville and Lexington, you will see miles of running board fence painted white or black. Behind the fence horses graze on grass growing from soil rich in limestone.

Those horses are big business. An agrarian society since Daniel Boone's time, Kentuckians put to good use the serendipitous mix of land and knowledge that made their place near perfect for raising horses.

As surely as men would race these horses, so too they would buy the good ones. To answer the demand for fast steeds, men went into business. They made their way in Boone's "dark and bloody ground" by breeding and selling racehorses.

Horses were first bred for racing in England sometime before 1654. That's when Oliver Cromwell banned racing. Racetracks had become meeting places for Cromwell's enemies.

From these breedings done in the name of seventeenth-century war came the thoroughbred. Maybe it all started on the deserts of Arabia, where, it is said, Mohammed let loose a herd of hot horses within sight of water. All ran toward it.

Then a trumpeter blew a battle call. Two stallions and five mares stopped and ran back to the trumpeter. From these obedient horses Mohammed bred the five great Arabian families.

As Mark Twain said of another matter, "Splendid legend. Splendid lie. Drive on."

TRACK OPEN
FOR TRAINING
6AM-10AM

Know Your Horse

There was a chill in the air during Derby Week of 1957, and the old wood-burning, potbellied stove in the tack room of Barn 26 at Churchill Downs was a source of comforting warmth. Late on Friday morning, a bit more than twenty-four hours before the 83rd Kentucky Derby, two men in campaign chairs huddled close to the old stove. The older man, built like a football tackle, was Plain Ben "B.A." Jones, the greatest trainer America ever produced and now, in his twilight years, general manager for Mrs. Gene Markey's Calumet Farm. The younger man was Horace "Jimmy" Jones, head trainer for Calumet Farm and son of Ben Jones. The Joneses had a problem. Calumet's brilliant colt Gen. Duke, conqueror of Bold Ruler in the Florida Derby and favored to win the Run for the Roses, would miss the race because of a broken foot. That left the Joneses with Iron Liege, a well-bred colt by Bull Lea out of Iron Maiden, a daughter of Triple Crown winner War Admiral. But for all of his pedigree, Iron Liege was no Gen. Duke.

As a final tightener for the Kentucky Derby, Jimmy Jones had entered Iron Liege in the Derby Trial Stakes on Tuesday of Derby Week. Only four days before the big race, it was a bit close for some trainers. But Ben Jones had prepped most of his six Kentucky Derby winners in the Trial and Jimmy Jones saw no reason to change the successful pattern. With Dave Erb in the saddle, Iron Liege had finished fifth. Now, as they sat around the stove at Barn 26, the Joneses were taking stock of what appeared to be a disastrous situation.

"Iron Liege should get some benefit out of the Trial," Ben said.

"Yes," Jimmy responded. "But he can't run the race he ran in the Trial. He [the colt] didn't care for that restraint. Bill Hartack will have to ride him, and he's got to let the colt run more of his own race. The only thing I feel good about is Hartack. He's never been riding better and he wants his first Derby very much."

The Derby Dream

On the eve of the Derby, Bill Shoemaker, who was engaged to ride Gallant Man in the race, and his agent, Harry Silbert, visited with the colt's owner, oilman Ralph Lowe, trainer Johnny Nerud, and some Texan friends at the Brown Hotel in Louisville. "Now that Shoe is here," Nerud said to Lowe, "you can tell him about the dream." Lowe explained that he had dreamed, a few days earlier, of his horse running in the Kentucky Derby. Suddenly, approaching the finish line, the jockey stood in the irons and the horse, his action disturbed by the movement, lost the race in a photo finish. "Now that I've heard the story, I'll be very careful about that," Shoemaker reassured the owner. "There's nothing to worry about now."

Two Dreams Come True

Federal Hill set the pace in the 83rd Kentucky Derby, with Bold Ruler racing second during the early stages under The Master, Eddie Arcaro, while Bill Hartack saved ground along the inside with Iron Liege in third position. Round Table, under Ralph Neves, was running fourth, and Gallant Man, going easily under Bill Shoemaker, was well back in the field of nine.

As Federal Hill began to tire near the eighth pole, Iron Liege took command. Gallant Man, in full stride now, raced third. With a bit more than a sixteenth of a mile remaining, Gallant Man, on the outside, drew even with Iron Liege and the crowd roared its appreciation as the drama unfolded on the track.

Approaching the sixteenth pole, Iron Liege and Gallant Man were head and head, locked in a furious duel. Shoemaker, on Gallant Man, rose for just an instant in the saddle and then sat down almost in a continuous motion, quickly aware of his error.

Apparently he had mistaken the sixteenth pole for the finish line.

When Shoe rose, Gallant Man did not visibly break stride. Once he regained his seat, Shoe pressed his mount, but at the finish it was Iron Liege in front by a nose, with Round Table a distant third, almost three lengths farther back, and three full lengths in front of Bold Ruler.

Hartack had won his first Derby and Calumet had won its sixth with its second-string colt. Ralph Lowe's bizarre dream had come true.

Outsmarting a Gypsy

Benjamin Allyn Jones was born in 1883 in Parnell, Missouri. He was raised on his parents' cattle farm and got his early education in a one-room schoolhouse his father had built. He grew up to be a big man with clear blue eyes, a smooth round face, a sharp mind, and a quick temper. Even as a boy, he was known as B.A.

After graduating from high school, he went to Colorado Agricultural College on a football scholarship. But after a couple of years, B.A. returned home to help his father with the operation of the farm. The only problem was that Ben Jones was more interested in horses than cattle.

At that time gypsies and their wagons crisscrossed the Midwest, selling everything from household goods to horses. In the spring of 1905, shortly after he'd married Etta McLaughlin, a local girl, B.A. saw a gypsy caravan pull into Parnell with some horses for sale. He liked a filly with an obvious knee problem and offered $100. The gypsy approved the deal with one stipulation: He had the option to buy the filly back the following spring for $150.

Jones patched up the filly, which he named Black Beauty, to the point where her knee was sound. The next spring the gypsy and his wagon returned to Parnell. When word reached Jones, he and Rebo Stites, a farmhand and friend, got busy. Rebo jabbed a nail into one of Black Beauty's feet, and when the gypsy arrived at the farm, the filly was hobbling pitifully. The gypsy shook his head and headed for his wagon. As the gypsy rode off, Jones pulled out the nail, cleansed the small wound with turpentine, and Black Beauty was as good as new. Jones had outsmarted a gypsy, no small achievement, and he and Rebo began to collect the fruit of their labors. They entered Black Beauty in match races at bush tracks and fair meetings throughout the region and collected on many a bet. Soon Ben Jones began to earn a reputation throughout the Midwest as a good man with a horse.

Father-and-Son Team

A gambler all his life, B.A. loved to shoot craps. He was rolling the dice in the old pig barn at the Jones farm on Thanksgiving night, November 24, 1906, when Rebo burst through the door and shouted, "Ben, you've got to go for the doctor now. The baby is being born!"

"Okay," Jones hollered back. "As soon as I make my point."

He threw a four, broke the game, and, stuffing $425 in his pocket, ran for the buckboard and made a hasty trip to fetch the doctor. The baby was named Horace Allyn Jones, after his grandfather, but quickly gained his lifelong nickname, Jimmy.

As B.A. continued to race his successful stable throughout the Midwest, Jimmy Jones grew up at home in Parnell, joining his father during summer vacations from school at racetracks in cities like Omaha and Louisville. Occasionally he would go by himself with a horse or two to small bush meetings near Parnell and try to win a race. Jimmy was the trainer, groom, blacksmith, exercise boy, and hotwalker on those expeditions.

In 1926 Jimmy took out a trainer's license and saddled his first winner, Nose Dive, at the Fair Grounds track on Gentilly Boulevard in New Orleans.

In the summer of 1932, at the height of the Depression, the Joneses, like everyone else, were struggling to meet expenses. It was at that time that Herbert Woolf, a prominent Kansas City merchant, asked Ben Jones to train his Woolford

Herbert Woolf, Ben and Jimmy Jones, and Eddie Arcaro on Lawrin in Winner's Circle of 1938 Derby

Farm stable. B.A. accepted and went to work almost immediately, while Jimmy Jones sold—and in a few cases, gave away—the remaining racing stock and broodmares.

When Jimmy rejoined B.A. at the racetrack, the fortunes of the Woolford Farm stable were on the upswing, thanks to B.A.'s expertise and the arrival of a new stallion, Insco.

A Colt for the Derby

In 1937 a colt named Lawrin, from one of Insco's first crops, joined the barn. A slow study, he showed very little at first, but then began to come to hand for the patient Ben Jones and won three of fifteen starts as a 2-year-old.

While Lawrin was hardly regarded as a leader of his generation, Ben Jones saw quality in him, took him to Miami that winter, and won Hialeah's Flamingo Stakes. A big, robust individual and a glutton with his feed, Lawrin improved with winter racing. After being shipped to Kentucky in the spring, however, Lawrin developed a foot abscess and missed some work. Calling on his considerable experience, Jones succeeded in correcting the problem, and Lawrin, right again, was pointed for the 64th Kentucky Derby.

If Lawrin had not had winter racing, he would not have been sufficiently fit, because of his foot problem, to make the mile and a quarter of the Run for the Roses. Even with winter racing, he badly needed some competition after his layoff. Jones decided on the Derby Trial, four days before the Derby. Outfitted with a set of bar shoes in front—one to give support to the recuperating foot and the other for balance—Lawrin, under Irving Anderson, finished a close second to The Chief, the 1–2 favorite. The Joneses were encouraged.

Two decisions were made. The bar shoes, which prevent a horse from digging in and doing his best, were removed. This represented a gamble, for Lawrin's fragile foot could go wrong, but all his life Ben Jones had gone for the brass ring. The other decision regarded a rider. Young Eddie Arcaro did not have a Derby mount. What he did have was a reputation as a daring and skillful jockey with a good sense of pace and the ability to think under pressure. This was to be one of racing's most successful pairings.

First Derby Win

The morning of Derby Day Ben Jones led Arcaro over every inch of the Churchill Downs track, discussing which parts were firm and which soft. Most important, Ben Jones said, "Stay off the rail at all costs."

Fighting Fox, winner of the Wood Memorial, was the 7–5 favorite in that 1938 Kentucky Derby. The second choice was the winner of the Blue Grass Stakes at Keeneland, Calumet Farm's Bull Lea. Lawrin was mildly regarded at 8–1. Although Ben Jones enjoyed a growing reputation, he had never won a Kentucky Derby. The same could be said about Arcaro.

Arcaro gave a perfect performance. He saved ground down the backstretch, brought Lawrin off the pace on the turn, and came along the rail to take the lead turning into the stretch. Then Arcaro asked for more from the game and generous colt, and got it. Lawrin had a three-length lead at the furlong pole and needed it all, for fatigue began to take its toll in the stretch drive. He bore out through the final sixteenth but held on to win by a length over Dauber. Lawrin had been prepared by a master and ridden by The Master, and that was enough to get the job done.

There was quite a scene in the winner's circle. Arcaro, whom Jones had cautioned to stay off the rail at all costs, had kept his mount on the rail most of the way. Thus he almost choked when he heard B.A. praise his ride to reporters.

"Rode him exactly like I told him," Jones said.

"We Want to Win the Derby"

A year later, in August 1939, Warren Wright, owner of Calumet Farm, then as now a showplace, met with Ben Jones and asked him to become his

trainer. Mrs. Wright put it even more bluntly. "We want to win the Kentucky Derby," she said.

Jones realized right away how serious the Wrights were and the extent of their resources. Wright's father, William M. Wright, had founded the Calumet Baking Powder Company and sold it, in 1928, for a reported $40 million, a vast sum at the time. Jones wasted no time in accepting the offer. He took over the stable, with Jimmy as his assistant, at the end of that month.

Know Your Horse

The following spring, with much of the world already at war, Calumet's 2-year-olds went into training. Two colts by the Epsom Derby winner Blenheim II looked like twins. One was named Easy Blend, who eventually became a cheap claimer. The other was Whirlaway.

A rugged colt with a long tail and a lot of fire in his eyes, Whirlaway quickly stepped to the head of his class. He was hard to handle and caused many problems for the Joneses, but when he galloped, he gave the impression of being tireless, of being able to run all day. Ben Jones quickly made an important decision: He would devote himself to Whirlaway and Jimmy would train all the other horses. Ben spent hours at his task every day, with the consummate patience that was his hallmark. Under the hot summer sun at Chicago's Arlington Park, B.A. would sit patiently on his pony, teaching Whirlaway to be calm, first in the starting gate and then on the track as other horses galloped past. Jones also discovered that what he taught Whirlaway in the mornings was exactly what he would get from him in the afternoons. Know your horse. It all came back to that.

Biding for Time

Whirlaway made progress. That August at Saratoga he won the traditional Saratoga Special and the prestigious Hopeful Stakes, the major 2-year-old feature of the meeting.

The Flamingo at Hialeah was the premier 3-year-old stakes race of the winter season, and Warren Wright wanted to win it with Whirlaway. Ben Jones, however, wanted the colt to have more time. So to stave off pressure, Jones announced that the colt had developed a splint, a bony growth on the side of a horse's lower leg.

Ben Jones, who had once fooled a gypsy, scorched the hair around Whirlaway's leg, simulating the appearance of treatment with a firing iron. The colt got the extra rest his trainer felt he needed.

A Battle of Wills

With Whirlaway supposedly on the sidelines and with the Hialeah meeting coming to a close, Warren Wright went off on a fishing trip to the Florida Keys. Reading the sports section of the *Miami Herald* one morning at dockside, Wright spotted Whirlaway's name in the Tropical Park entries for the day's program.

Ordering a car and driver, Wright dressed quickly and headed for Tropical Park in Coral Gables. He was adamant that Whirlaway be scratched.

"This is a mile-and-a-quarter horse," Wright said. "It is ridiculous to run him in a five-and-a-half-furlong race."

"I'm not going to scratch him," said B.A., getting red in the face. "I'm the trainer. This is my way of training, and I think we should run him!"

Tempers had not cooled by race time, but Whirlaway came onto the track full of verve and looking a picture. He made his usual late run from far back and got up in the final strides to win.

Warren Wright was still smouldering, but as one friend after another came by the box to congratulate him, he began to calm down. Finally he told the Joneses, "I'm never going to train another horse. From now on you fellows are in charge. Use your own judgment and do what you think is best."

An Experiment That Worked

Whirlaway was shipped to Lexington to run in the Blue Grass Stakes at Keeneland. Our Boots, the 2-year-old champion of 1940, was the winner, but

Whirlaway was obviously the better horse. Feeling good, he was all over the racetrack, and Wendell Eads, his rider, was either unable or unwilling to control him.

The Joneses decided to try Whirlaway again in the Derby Trial, hoping that another prep race would straighten him out, but the Trial was a repetition of the Blue Grass.

Ben Jones tested Whirlaway in a one-eyed blinker, a cup that covers the outside eye. With a one-eyed blinker, a horse is afraid to run out where he can't see. There is no cup over the inside eye, so the horse can see the rail and the horses racing inside of him.

One other change was made. Eddie Arcaro was engaged to ride Whirlaway. On the morning before the Derby, Ben Jones had Arcaro out early for a frightening experiment.

Jones stationed himself on his pony in midstretch, three or four feet off the inner rail, and instructed Arcaro, during the blowout, to send Whirlaway through that narrow opening. Jones wanted Whirlaway to experience control and to go where his jockey led him. He also wanted to convince Arcaro that Whirlaway's terrible reputation for high jinks was no longer justified. He wanted Eddie to ride with confidence.

"I could see that old man just sitting there on his pony," Arcaro said later. "I was bearing down on him full tilt and was scared to death that we'd have a collision that would kill the both of us. But B.A. never moved a muscle and Whirlaway slipped through the narrow opening as pretty as you please, and then I knew we had a hell of a chance at the Derby."

Whirlaway won by eight lengths, and to this day no horse has won America's most coveted racing prize by a greater margin. Coming from far back in a field of eleven, Whirlaway raced on the inside down the backstretch and moved nicely between horses entering the stretch. Then, with his long tail streaming behind him, he left his pursuers in his wake, setting a track record of 2:01⅖ for the mile

Jimmy Jones

and a quarter. It was a mark that was to stand for twenty-one years.

Whirlaway went on to win the Preakness and Belmont, capturing the Triple Crown for Calumet. He was named Horse of the Year for 1941 and 1942, a year in which many tracks closed because of America's involvement in World War II.

A Wartime Derby Winner

In 1943 Jimmy Jones was commissioned as a lieutenant in the Coast Guard. However, the next spring Lieutenant Jones took leave of his duties for a few days to assist his father at Churchill Downs with Calumet's Kentucky Derby entry, Pensive. Lightly raced at 2, Pensive was moderately regarded at 7–1 for the Kentucky Derby, which had a red-hot favorite in Greentree Stable's Stir Up, ridden by Arcaro. Stir Up, however, was far from a good horse. In fact, the Derby field was quite ordinary, and Ben Jones felt he could win the race. Pensive came from far back under Conn McCreary in a field of sixteen to win the Kentucky Derby easily by 4½ lengths. Pensive also won the Preakness, but in doing so ran down and burned his heels. The injury hampered his preparation for the Belmont Stakes, which he lost by half a length, denying Calumet a second Triple Crown winner. At least for a while.

Top of the Class

The young horses raised at Calumet Farm were graded like schoolchildren, the criteria including appearance, conformation, soundness, and smoothness of stride. In 1946 two of the forty yearlings received high marks. Sons of Bull Lea, their names were Citation and Coaltown.

Citation, out of Hydroplane II by Hyperion, came to hand surprisingly early and won his first three starts.

Meanwhile, Coaltown was advancing toward his first start when he fell on the track one morning, in the middle of a gallop, and hemorrhaged severely. For a few days his status was perilous, but he

managed to pull through. He was sent back to the farm in Kentucky, where he remained until it was time to go south to Florida for the winter. Citation concluded his 2-year-old career in November by winning the Pimlico Futurity.

That February at Hialeah Jimmy Jones boldly tested Citation against the nation's top older speed horses in the Seminole Handicap. When the colt won easily, Jones knew he had a great horse. Citation similarly trounced his 3-year-old rivals in the Everglades and Flamingo Stakes, establishing himself as a hot favorite for the Kentucky Derby.

A Two-Horse Race

Ben Jones had taken a division of the stable to Keeneland and was delighted with Coaltown's progress. The speedy horse had gone from strength to strength through the spring and had won Keeneland's prestigious Blue Grass Stakes in a track-record 1:49⅕ with Newbold Leroy Pierson in the irons. Calumet had a second Derby contender. Five days later Citation won the Derby Trial with Eddie Arcaro up, and the stature of the two Calumet colts frightened away many prospective opponents for the 74th Kentucky Derby on May 1, 1948. There were only six starters, with the Calumet Farm entry a prohibitive 2–5 favorite. Although Jimmy Jones had developed Citation, it was decided that B.A. would be listed as his trainer for the Kentucky Derby. A victory would tie Jones, at four winners each, with "Derby Dick" Thompson, who had trained for Colonel E.R. Bradley in the 1920s and 1930s. The Wrights wanted that honor for the man who had brought international renown to their farm, and Jimmy was quick to agree.

The Joneses' strategy was for Coaltown to set the pace in the Derby. When the track came up sloppy on Derby Day, Arcaro was cautioned not to permit Citation to race too close to Coaltown. Were Citation to press his competitive stablemate, Coaltown would try harder and would harm his chances of finishing second.

With the first half mile in a lively :46⅗, Coaltown, with Pierson up, opened a lead of six lengths, and both Jimmy Jones and Eddie Arcaro were wondering to themselves if B.A. had pulled a fast one. Arcaro went to his whip earlier than planned, and Citation, who had been waiting for the word, quickly sliced Coaltown's lead in half. Seeing the response he received, Eddie regained confidence in his colt and took Citation back in hand. He permitted the big bay colt to go to the front on his own courage leaving the quarter-pole, and once in the lead, Citation drew away. He led by two lengths with a furlong remaining and won, apparently with something left, by 3½ lengths, with the game Coaltown second.

Citation went on to win the Preakness and Belmont Stakes to give Calumet its second sweep of the Triple Crown. His 3-year-old season, with nineteen victories in twenty starts and one controversial second, has been called the finest such campaign by an American horse in this century.

A Surprise Kentucky Derby Winner

Calumet had another Kentucky Derby winner in 1949, but whereas Citation and Coaltown went off at 2–5, Ponder's odds were 16–1. A son of the 1944 Kentucky Derby winner, Pensive, the colt was out of Miss Rushin, a Blenheim II mare who had never won a race. It appeared, at first, that Ponder was going to take after his dam.

Ponder was 3 before he finally reached the winner's circle in a seven-furlong race at Gulfstream Park, finishing as if he might be best suited by a distance of ground. He showed improvement at Keeneland that spring and was then transferred to Churchill Downs, where he finished second in the Derby Trial Stakes to Fred W. Hooper's Olympia, the 4–5 favorite for the 75th Run for the Roses.

As anticipated, Olympia set the pace in the Derby with Ponder racing last of fourteen starters for the first half mile. With Steve Brooks in the saddle, Ponder began to pick up momentum around the turn. After the first mile Olympia was finished, and Capot, well placed under Ted Atkinson, took

command. At the eighth pole he was three lengths in front, with Palestinian and Ponder behind him, the Calumet colt on the outside. Through the stretch Capot was unable to stand off Ponder's run, and the Calumet colt won by three lengths in 2:04⅕. Capot was second, 4½ lengths ahead of Palestinian. Ben Jones was credited with an unprecedented fifth victory in the Run for the Roses, and Warren Wright had another golden trophy for his huge case at Calumet Farm. This was a cup he had coveted, for, emblematic of the 75th Derby, it was encrusted with a semicircular row of diamonds.

It was to be his final major triumph. Warren Wright died at his winter home in Miami on December 31, 1950. Mrs. Wright, equally dedicated to the stable, took charge of Calumet.

Handling a Handful

Mrs. Wright remarried in 1952. Her new husband was Admiral Gene Markey, a film producer, author, raconteur, and a most charming man. Calumet won the Kentucky Derby again in 1952, with Hill Gail. This talented but overly nervous colt was, like Citation, a son of Bull Lea. However, he took after his dam's side of the family when it came to deportment. Jane Gail, his mother, had been fast and erratic. Her dam, in turn, was the furiously high-strung Lady Higloss.

Hill Gail showed his ability at 2 by winning the Arlington Futurity and finishing second in the Washington Park Futurity. But as he turned 3 and began to prepare for the Santa Anita Derby, he proved a handful for Jimmy Jones. Hill Gail was strong as a bull, and no equipment tried was equal to his temperament and willfulness.

As a boy on the farm in Missouri, Jones had on occasion been required to deal with obstreperous workhorses. His technique had been to hitch the difficult horse between two large and well-mannered ones and set the doubletrees in a manner that put most of the workload on the horse who was acting up. In short order the horse would tire himself and learn to behave.

Ben and Jimmy Jones in 1957 accompanying Bill Hartack on Gen. Duke.

Jones located a strong and experienced cowboy, Slim Whitman, who was ponying horses for a living in Santa Anita. Jimmy and Slim would accompany Hill Gail to the track in the morning, each alongside on a pony, and each holding a stout shank attached to Hill Gail's bridle. Calumet's most experienced exercise rider, Albert Edward "Pinky" Brown, would be on Hill Gail.

All three men used their strength to control Hill Gail in his morning gallops. After a brief period, Jones dismissed Whitman and went out by himself to help Pinky Brown handle Hill Gail. Then Jones dropped out and left Pinky on his own.

The preparation proved effective. Hill Gail won the Santa Anita Derby, came to Keeneland to beat older horses in the Phoenix Handicap (America's oldest stakes race), and then won the Derby Trial at Churchill Downs in a track record of 1:35⅖ for the mile.

A short-priced favorite (11–10) for the Kentucky Derby of 1952, Hill Gail had the familiar Eddie Arcaro in the irons as he faced fifteen opponents. Hill Gail was first out of the gate from post one, but after half a mile, Bayard Sharp's Hannibal was in front by two lengths. Arcaro sensed that Hill Gail was about to pitch a tantrum. Instead of reacting to the colt's temperament, The Master called the tune. He asked Hill Gail for everything he had in him and the colt had neither the time nor the energy to act up. He just kept running and was near exhaustion when he passed the finish line two lengths clear of Dixiana's Sub Fleet.

Ben Jones, who had saddled Hill Gail, had his sixth Kentucky Derby victory, five of them for Calumet Farm. It was to be his last as a trainer.

A Courageous Colt

Jimmy Jones saddled Iron Liege for that memorable Derby victory in 1957 and came back in 1958 to win the Derby again with Tim Tam. One of the most underrated horses of our time, Tim Tam (by Tom Fool out of champion Two Lea) was out of the money only once in his career.

After his Derby win, Tim Tam won the Preakness and was an odds-on favorite in the Belmont for a sweep of the Triple Crown. He was moving to challenge the victorious Cavan near the quarter-pole when he suddenly shattered a bone in his left foreleg. Despite what must have been intense pain, he continued on to finish second in a performance that was the exemplar of courage in a thoroughbred racehorse. Subsequently, a masterful operation enabled Tim Tam to retire to stud.

Jones Era Ends

The man they called Plain Ben Jones died of complications from diabetes on June 13, 1961. At a memorial service in Lexington, Kentucky, attended by racing notables, he was hailed as the greatest trainer America ever produced.

In 1961, the year his father died, Jimmy Jones performed his greatest training feat. Without a star of consequence in the stable, he took Calumet to the top of the earnings list as America's leading owner. Cleverly placing his horses where they were most effective and utilizing his resources to the maximum, he demonstrated great skill as a manager and as a trainer, and reflected credit on himself as well as on the master who had taught him the profession.

In August 1964, Jimmy Jones was offered the post of Monmouth Park's director of racing. He accepted, and on October 1, 1964, a little more than twenty-five years after he and his father had started working at Calumet Farm, Jimmy Jones moved into his office at Monmouth Park and started a second career.

The Jones era at the Kentucky Derby, a remarkable saga encompassing eight victories by father and son in America's most coveted race, was officially over.

The best time at a racetrack is first light. Dawn is full of promise and mystery. "Ain't nowhere else to be, 'cept with horses in the morning," said Woody Stephens, the great trainer.

In the morning mist, trainers first test a horse's ability. They teach their athletes to win.

Exercise riders come back from the work with some intelligence for the trainer. Maybe the horse shies from other horses. Or refuses instructions. No, he is not playing out there. Yes, he does understand this is work.

There are many pieces of the puzzle that a trainer must put into place before it's time to go racing. Does the colt run better in a snaffle bit? If he looks around, blinker him. If that's not the answer, let's try a shadow roll. To straighten out Gate Dancer (overleaf), trainer Jack Van Berg needed a shadow roll, blinkers, and earmuffs.

And still you don't know the ultimate answer. Can he win? Only the race can tell you, for only the race tests the horse's will. "You can't cut 'em open and look at their heart," Van Berg once said. "They gotta show you by running."

Don't be misled by the pony rider's fringed chaps and shiny spurs. His job is difficult and dangerous. He's there to help control rambunctious thoroughbreds at morning workouts which can stretch into hours of drudgery.

Only that hard morning workout produces the afternoon's thrills. For at bottom, the track is a nitty-gritty place where the rewards go to those who get their hands dirty, those who work their leather boots into the straw and mud.

It's a delicate balance. While stretching each horse to his full ability, trainers must work cautiously. Horses are half-ton creatures running on breadstick legs. Trainers fear the one bad step that can end a runner's racing days.

Some horses walk. Others come to the track's river of sunlight to work out. There is serious hard work to be done here. The exercise rider is up in the irons, soon to demand that the horse run. His hands on the reins, his body in balance, the rider knows what he wants from the horse. And if he doesn't get it, he'll reach to the back pocket of his faded jeans.

Derby horses at work the week of their biggest race. Of maybe 50,000 foals in their crop, just a handful make it this far. Of the eight seen here, only Alysheba won the Derby.

Workouts usually are private affairs, of interest only to trainers, riders, and clockers. That changes for the Derby. Before dawn, men with TV cameras come to the track. Newspaper reporters crowd around the trainers, whose private world becomes public.

A trainer watches the work from the backside rail. Later he walks the horse to his barn and rubs a hand over the animal's legs. He does this gently, feeling for the heat of infection, also checking the bone for flaws. A trainer, a horseman, and a celebrity this Derby week, he also is a diagnostician.

It's all a mystery, this work in the morning. Whatever the result, there is argument over its meaning. A fast workout may mean the horse is ready to run. But what if the Derby is four days away? Will he keep that fitness the rest of the week?

Veteran horsemen laughed in 1971 when Canonero II arrived at Churchill Downs debilitated by his exhausting trip from Caracas. But they didn't laugh on Derby Day, when Canonero II circled his field to win.

Eleven days before the 1986 Derby, Bill Shoemaker arose at 5:00 A.M. to work out a filly. Great jockeys don't do much of this. But Shoe needed to know what he could learn best in the morning.

Shoemaker, on the filly, thought of Ferdinand, his Derby horse. He heard the colt's breathing. "He went by me, whoooosh," Shoemaker said.

Ferdinand and Bill Shoemaker won. Said trainer Charlie Whittingham, then seventy-three: "Never winning the Derby didn't make me want to shoot myself. I won races everywhere. But, gee. Everybody knows the Kentucky Derby. You say, 'Geez, I did do a helluva thing.'"

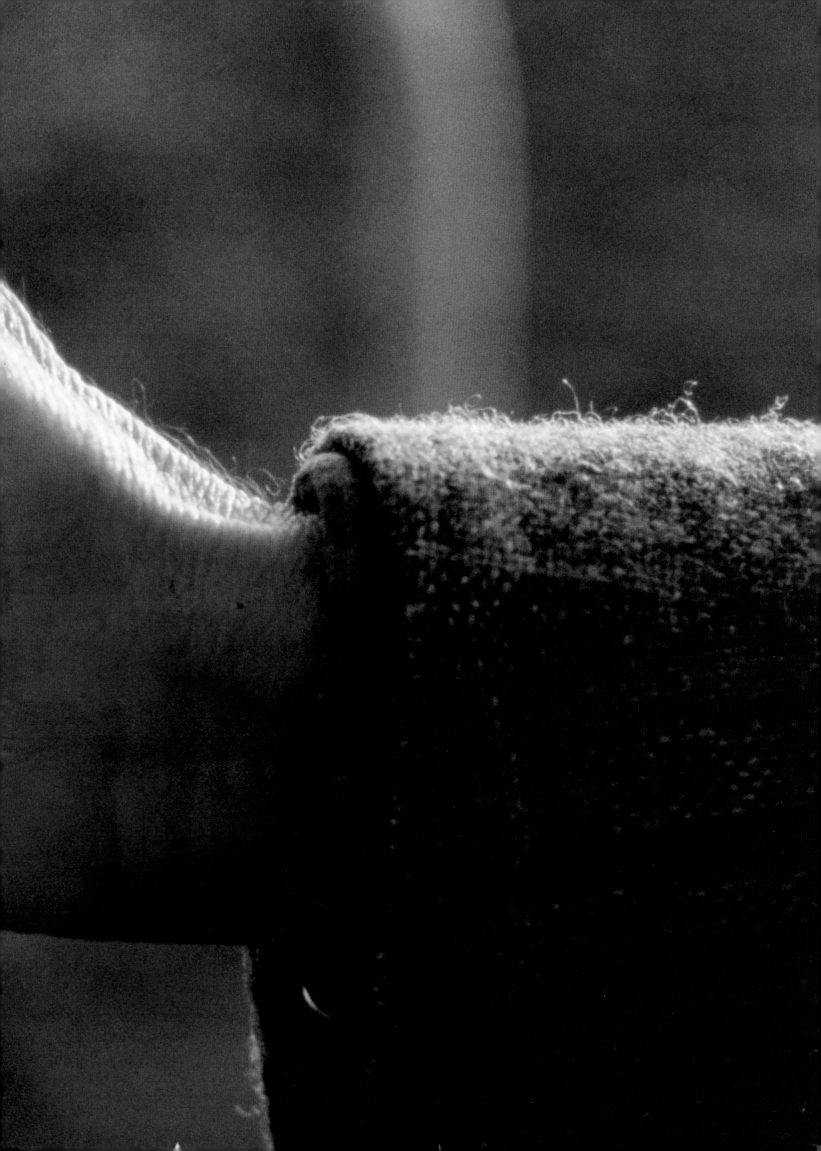

Charlie Whittingham

William H. Turner, Jr.

John Longden

Grover G. Delp

Lazaro S. Barrera

Lucien Laurin

Johnny Nerud

Hirsch Jacobs

Woodford C. Stephens

Max Hirsch

D. Wayne Lukas

Jack Van Berg

John P. Campo

Eddie Neloy

LeRoy Jolley

Horatio A. Luro; overleaf, the Jones Boys flanking Bill Hartack

The River City Festival

t was 1:00 A.M. on the Saturday morning before the 1953 Kentucky Derby when Eddie Arcaro and Bill Shoemaker entered Dick Andrade's suite at the old Brown Hotel in Louisville for a couple of "shooters" before retiring. Andrade, a Texas oil man and bon vivant, was one of many notable hosts throughout the city on the eve of America's greatest horse race. Andrade's parties, however, were usually distinguished by a certain quality of the unexpected. As Arcaro and Shoemaker, two of racing's finest jockeys, walked into a living room jammed with prominent racing personalities from all parts of the United States, they shook their heads in astonishment.

Walking over to inspect them was . . . a horse! Andrade's fertile imagination had reasoned that nothing would better suit a Kentucky Derby party than an equine guest. With money no object, Andrade had arranged for a pony to attend the party. The pony's trainer received a couple of hundred for his participation. Also on the payroll was the pony's groom, who outfitted the animal with rubber shoes to lessen the impact of the guest's presence on the Brown Hotel carpeting and to spirit him up the freight elevator with the cooperation of its elevator operator—who had been paid off handsomely as well. More money went to a companion of the groom, who drove a small, one-horse trailer to the rear entrance of the hotel.

Talk-of-the-Town Parties

The entire matter cost Andrade about $500, but his party was the talk of the town for years afterward in a city that parties wildly on the eve of its day in the national spotlight. Derby Eve parties, hosted by prominent Louisvillians of all types, were renowned for their revelry and ostentation. Size, too. John Y. Brown, Jr., a fast-food restaurateur who later became governor of Kentucky, hosted as many as 500 guests under huge tents at the home in suburban Louisville that he shared with his first wife, Ellie. Troupes of uniformed attendants met the cars and limousines, which arrived in a steady stream, and escorted guests to cocktail bars and elaborate sit-down dinners while two orchestras alternated with appropriate music. Brown owned Louisville's professional basketball team in those days, and his players, some of them seven feet tall, lent a bizarre counterpoint to the colorful scene. For diversity of guest lists, none of the Louisville parties could match those assembled by the insurance executive Edward J. McGrath and his wife, Eva. On one memorable occasion at the McGraths' expansive home near Cherokee Park, a buffet line leading to large platters of delicacies included Senator Hubert Humphrey of Minnesota, New York Jets president David "Sonny" Werblin, restaurateur Toots Shor, running back Tucker Fredrickson of the New York Giants, sportscaster Jack Whitaker, film and television star Telly Savalas, two former governors of Kentucky, three Air Force generals, and an Indian chieftain from Nevada.

The Chief was an expert horseman who had fallen on hard times and had come to Louisville with a Las Vegas attorney, Mike Hines. Hines owned a thoroughbred named One Eyed Tom, who had never started in a race but had been brought to Louisville to run in the Kentucky Derby. In those days, if you paid a nomination fee of $100 plus starting charges, your horse was eligible to run the race. The Churchill Downs stewards, however, aghast at One Eyed Tom's lack of racing experience, insisted he break out of the gate for them one morning during Derby Week. No sooner had he come out than One Eyed Tom made a sharp left-hand turn, heading for the rail. Had there been other horses breaking inside of him, he would have wiped out half the Derby field. The stewards said, "No, thanks," but Hines and his trainer decided to stay over to see the big race.

The Chief was a man of few words, and most of

them were in his native tongue. While Hines mixed easily with other guests at the McGrath party, the Chief went through the buffet line, obtained a large glass of firewater, borrowed a blanket from a hall closet, and proceeded to the McGraths' front lawn. There he spread the blanket, set his food and drink in front of him, and with appropriate dignity enjoyed his party sitting cross-legged in splendid privacy. He made a striking figure—especially to late-arriving guests, many of whom had already had a drink or two and could not believe their eyes.

More "Bust Out" Parties

But then, this was Derby Week, like Mardi Gras in New Orleans—and almost everything was possible in the carefree 1950s and 1960s. For several years hotel "parades" were the rage. Spirited young men and women—and many an older Kentucky Colonel caught up in the excitement of the occasion— collected garbage can lids and other metal objects and wended their way through the halls of the old Kentucky Hotel, the Seelbach, and the Watterson, beating their makeshift instruments to a fare-thee-well. These musical interludes, usually played past midnight, were not always well received by those guests who had retired early in anticipation of a strenuous Derby Day. Hotel managements were broad-minded, however, and drew the line only when paraders would occasionally carry furniture to the roof and throw it to the streets below.

The railroad yards were also the scene of much conviviality. In the 1920s, the sagacious Colonel Matt Winn, the Louisville tailor who had become chief executive officer of Churchill Downs, persuaded several railroad lines, particularly those with routes to Louisville from New York and Chicago, to buy blocks of tickets to the Kentucky Derby and promote package deals with their customers. Many of those who came to the Derby by train used the sleeping cars as their hotel, and eventually the sidings were jammed. As the popularity of the Derby grew, many wealthy Americans with their own railway cars joined the party, until the railroad yards resembled a small city. Important guests were entertained and considerable corporate business was accomplished in this unlikely setting. Among the many celebrities who "trained in" for the Derby were Prince Rainier of Monaco, George Jessel, Gene Tunney, Al Jolson, Vice President Charles Curtis, and New York's flamboyant Mayor Jimmy Walker.

Unforgettable Characters

This was the era of "character patrons," those fans who gloried in bizarre individuality on Derby Day. Among the regulars were an elderly man who dressed as Uncle Sam; the Hat Lady, who attempted to outdo herself each year with outrageous creations featuring roses, twin steeples, and horses; and the incredible Diamond Jim Moran. Mr. Moran, from New Orleans, carried his appreciation of precious stones to the extreme. He had diamond rings on every finger, diamonds imbedded in all his front teeth, and diamonds sewn prominently to his clothing. On a sunny day his glittering presence in the popular finish-line box sections F and G literally dazzled the eye.

The Infield Crowd

Churchill Downs's infield has become today's most colorful scene of celebration. "Discovered" by young America in the late sixties through the mysterious "young boy network," it has become an annual event along with such occasions as the Super Bowl, spring break in Fort Lauderdale, and the Indianapolis 500. Beginning on the Friday night before the Derby's traditional "first Saturday in May," crowds of young men and women, many of them in campers, vans, and flatbed trucks of various configurations, begin to line up on Longfield Avenue, paralleling the stable area.

Although there is usually some partying through the night, the Louisville police keep the noise levels under control because one side of Longfield Avenue is a residential area and the other side is home to the valuable Derby horses. When the infield area

The Duke and Duchess of Windsor arrive at the 1951 Derby.

gates open at 8:00 A.M., however, all restraints are swept aside and waves of people flow in. Patrons have their choice of almost the entire infield. Personal areas are staked out, small tents are erected, and serious partying begins. While alcoholic beverages are officially prohibited from being carried into the infield, numerous and imaginative attempts have been made to thwart the ushers and security guards at the gates—and some have succeeded. One group got through with what appeared to be a heavy sofa. The reason for its weight was that a compartment containing several cases of beer had been built underneath the seats!

When streaking was a fad, the Churchill Downs infield had several spectacular exhibitions. Perhaps the most notable was in 1974 during the 100th Kentucky Derby, at which Princess Margaret of England was among the guests of honor. During a lull between races, one of the infield celebrants, wearing only his birthday suit, attempted to climb the flagpole. Churchill Downs officials, foreseeing that possibility, had carefully greased the pole, but the climber rose surprisingly high before sliding down into the arms of the police.

That Centennial Derby, won by John Olin's Cannonade, attracted a record field of twenty-three and a record crowd of 163,628. Neither mark is likely to be achieved again. Traffic in the race was so severe that Churchill Downs's board of directors adopted a rule to limit future fields to twenty horses, based on earnings. Everyone agreed that the day's infield crowd of over 100,000 was also too large. Recently, the higher infield ticket price has limited the size of the crowd.

Other ticket prices have been raised as well, yet the demand is greater than ever, and a good seat to the Kentucky Derby is one of the toughest tickets in sports to acquire.

Visiting the Derby

The character of the Derby crowd has changed over the years. Whereas patrons arrived by train or car in the 1950s and 1960s, they began arriving by plane in the 1970s, and that trend has broadened steadily. Progress in air travel has made it feasible to fly into Louisville on the morning of the race and return home in early evening. As the Derby has also become a popular corporate plum, many corporations buy blocks of tickets for favored customers, personnel, or politicians.

Those Derby fans who arrive several days prior to the race usually book into such midtown hotels as the new Galt House East, the Galt House, the Hyatt Regency, or a handsomely refurbished hostelry of the past such as the Brown or the Seelbach. Those motoring to the Derby often prefer suburban hotels such as the Executive Inn, the Executive West, or several large Holiday Inns along the Watterson Expressway. The majority of the hotels and motels retain a three-day package plan that has prevailed for many years, and rates average several hundred dollars a day. This rate structure has encouraged the fly-in, fly-out strategy of many fans, though most hotels are fully booked nonetheless.

Large fleets of taxicabs cluster around the hotels on Derby morning to transport thousands to Churchill Downs via the one-way street system organized by the Louisville Police Department. These one-way streets leading to the historic Downs are reversed in late afternoon, and the Derby crowd, no matter how large, is dispersed in rapid order. So efficient is the Louisville system that the traffic departments of many major police forces in America and abroad have visited the Derby to observe it in action.

Famed Derby Eve Hosts

With many visitors on hand only for Derby Day, the character of Derby celebrations has changed, too. Derby Eve parties are still held throughout the city, but they seem much more sedate and poised than the "bust out" parties of the past. The trend is away from heavy foods and whiskey to light meals and white wine.

There is still a great deal of Derby spirit to be

found, however, in nearby Lexington, the thoroughbred capital of America, some seventy miles east of Louisville. There the grand blast of all Derby parties is hosted by Anita Madden and her husband, Preston, who operate the famed Hamburg Place breeding farm, which has been in the Madden family for almost a century. Anita Madden's annual party, enjoyed by some 500 guests, is a furious pastiche of lights, music, dancing, celebrities, decor, and—above all—upbeat tempo. Many stage and screen stars attend as the Maddens' guests and then are bused to the Derby the next day with a roadside respite for fried chicken and other traditional Southern dishes.

Another celebrated Lexington Derby Eve host and hostess are Mr. and Mrs. Cornelius Vanderbilt Whitney, who attract a more sedate crowd to the family farm on the Paris Pike. Members of Congress, royalty, and film stars of yesteryear such as Ginger Rogers and Gregory Peck are often found on the Whitney guest list. For dancing, "Smoke Gets in Your Eyes" is heard far more often than "Bad, Bad Leroy Brown," a standard at the Madden celebration.

Combining Business and Pleasure

For many racing executives, Derby Week is a busman's holiday during which they feel they can see more people and get more work done than at any other time of the year. Accordingly, they visit with one another at such events as the Kentucky Thoroughbred Owners and Breeders dinner on Tuesday night at the Hyatt Regency, the National Turf Writers Association dinner Wednesday night at the Galt House, or the Churchill Downs Derby party Thursday night at the Galt House East. On Friday morning, racetrack executives make a traditional pilgrimage to the Downs for training hours, where they can exchange pleasantries with one another and chat with Derby trainers and owners in hopes of inducing them to other important stakes at their tracks.

The corporate image is strong in Louisville Derby Eve and Derby Day. Companies with guests on hand Friday night book large tables at the city's best-known restaurants, such as Hasenour's, Casa Grisanti, and Masterson's, where those with less clout may wait as long as two hours for a table. The majority of the top establishments have special limited menus to facilitate the speedy turnover of diners. On Derby Day, corporations that participate in a sponsorship arrangement may entertain their guests and clients in handsomely appointed tents, in a landscaped area leading from the Longfield Avenue clubhouse gate. Gaily colored umbrellas and traditional jug bands add just the right touch to the proceedings as guests drink, dine, wager at nearby windows, and follow the racing action on monitors located in each tent.

Kentucky Derby Festival

For Louisvillians, Derby Week is nonstop festivity, with time at a premium, menus to plan, guests to greet, and mint to gather for juleps. The city of Louisville takes its Derby seriously, and many civic and governmental groups collaborate in planning and consummating the annual Kentucky Derby Festival, one of the largest such celebrations in the United States and now including some seventy events. At one time the Pegasus Parade and the Kentucky Colonels Banquet were the only major items on the agenda. In recent years, however, the success of the Festival has fed on itself and the program has lengthened to ten days.

The Festival gets under way on the Friday preceding Derby Week with the "They're Off" luncheon at the Galt House East, sponsored by the Brown-Forman Corporation. As many as 2,000 people attend this luncheon, which features a prominent guest speaker. Occasionally the speaker makes news with his remarks, as was the case in 1982, when the Lexington breeder John Gaines announced details of a proposed "Super Bowl" of racing, an afternoon of championship sport in the fall with seven events and a minimum purse of $1 million. His idea, the Breeders' Cup, is now a

EARLY TIMES

TURF CLASSIC

presents

the 1987
Kentucky Derby Press Party

Thursday, April 30
8:00 p.m.

showcase of racing and includes international participants.

The Saturday before the Derby, Churchill Downs opens its spring meeting, and that tradition alone is cause for celebration throughout the community. In recent years, the Kentucky Derby Festival has augmented the opening day with such events as a soccer tournament, a bass fishing contest on the Ohio River, and a hot-air balloon race.

A new celebration is the Kentucky Derby Museum Gala, a glamorous black-tie dinner-dance at Churchill Downs, sponsored by the Kentucky Derby Museum.

On Sunday the Kentucky Derby Festival features an event in Cherokee Park sponsored by Louisville's Pepsi-Cola Bottlers and South Central Bell. The family-oriented activities include picnics, entertainment by popular music groups, and an army sky-diving exhibition. For those who prefer an afternoon of gospel music, Kentucky Fried Chicken sponsors a concert at Shawnee Park.

Events follow one another with stunning precision during Derby Week. On Monday night, the Knights of Columbus Charity Dinner, honoring racing and media personalities, attracts crowds of 1,000 and more to the Galt House East, with the governor of Kentucky and the mayor of Louisville invariably in attendance. Monday also features a golf tournament and a square-dancing exhibition. Tuesday's main festivities are the colorful "Run for the Rosé" held in midtown, with waiters and waitresses from many restaurants racing across a plaza with trays of wine-filled glasses; and the Derby Trainers' Dinner in the evening at the Hyatt Regency Hotel, sponsored by the Kentucky Thoroughbred Owners and Breeders Association.

The Great Steamboat Race between the *Belle of Louisville* and the *Delta Queen* from Cincinnati begins Wednesday at 5:00 P.M. Tens of thousands line the banks of the Ohio River as the two steamers go up the river for several miles and then make a tight turn back to the finish line. Prominent guests invited aboard the two ships wave to the crowds,

while the public on the Louisville side of the river roots for the *Belle* and those on the Indiana side cheer for the *Queen*. The winning ship receives the coveted prize of a set of gilded elk's antlers. Sponsored by Southern Comfort, this race is one of the most popular Derby Festival events.

The Starting Lineup

Attention is focused on the Derby Thursday morning when Derby entries are taken and the field is drawn. Churchill Downs's racing secretary conducts the draw in the Kentucky Derby Museum while Derby horse owners, trainers, jockeys, breeders, and the press gather to analyze the merits of inside and outside post positions. Ed McGrath, famed for his colorful Derby Eve parties, hosts a lavish breakfast on the site of the old paddock. Kentucky ham, eggs, grits, and biscuits are served by white-jacketed waiters from the Harry M. Stevens catering organization to more than 1,000 guests. McGrath also provides a useful souvenir to each guest, such as a pen.

As the excitement of Derby Week spreads through Louisville, the annual Pegasus Parade on Broadway begins at 5:30 Thursday afternoon. A Kentucky celebrity from the stage, screen, or television is usually the Grand Marshal, and as many as 250,000 people line Broadway to cheer the floats, marching bands, and equestrian units. Later in the evening Philip Morris USA sponsors the Festival of Stars, including country-and-western personalities and rock groups, at the Kentucky State Fair and Exposition Center near the airport.

The Kentucky Oaks

Friday is the traditional date of the Kentucky Oaks, the filly counterpart of the Kentucky Derby, and it has become a major attraction. Crowds of between 50,000 and 60,000 gather at Churchill Downs to watch the best 3-year-old fillies from all over the country compete in the rich and prestigious Grade I feature. Because Derby Day traffic schedules are not yet in effect, long lines of cars move at a leisurely pace as the track's parking lots empty in late afternoon, and hostesses have learned to get their parties under way later than usual.

A different sort of event, Derby Eve Jam, takes place that evening at the Kentucky State Fair and Exposition Center, where popular rock groups participate in a giant concert that attracts thousands of young Louisvillians and Derby visitors.

The Kentucky Colonels Banquet highlights Friday's program, with more than 1,000 guests in formal attire dining and dancing at the Galt House East. While many Louisvillians entertain at home or in restaurants Friday evening, out-of-town Derby guests who are members of the Colonels, a highly motivated charitable organization, make up the majority at this traditional banquet. A prominent guest speaker, usually from the world of entertainment, helps to lighten the evening with his remarks.

Derby Day

To be sure, Derby Day is a celebration in itself. It has become a custom for the governor to entertain at the mansion in Frankfort, the state capital, with a typical Derby breakfast of eggs, Kentucky ham, grits, and beaten biscuits. Invitations go out to Kentuckians prominent in many fields, and between 1,000 and 2,000 guests are served in large tents on the grounds of the mansion, with the first family greeting each guest individually in a receiving line. Churchill Downs is about an hour away by car or bus, but nobody hurries.

Post time for the first race on Derby Day is exactly 11:30 A.M., and for those who have partied vigorously all week it is an early call to arms. Derby horsemen, who come out at 6:00 A.M. for a final look at their horses, are usually back at their home or hotel for a nap, nerves permitting. They will return to the barn about 3:00 P.M. and wait quietly with their horses, rather than sit in their boxes and endure endless questioning by nervous owners and their guests.

As the first race gets under way, the infield is packed with young people, the grandstand is filling rapidly, and the early members of the clubhouse crowd are beginning to arrive. In large dining rooms on the second level of the sprawling stands, a Derby breakfast is served by the Harry M. Stevens Company from a limited menu featuring filet mignon, chicken, and corned beef hash. In pleasant weather, the area behind the stands is jammed as racegoers munch on popcorn, enjoy the beauty of the formal tulip garden, chat with friends, and exchange information. Between races the crowd is restless, some patrons remaining in their seats to handicap the next race from the past performances listed in the *Daily Racing Form* while others adjourn to the paddock to inspect the horses that will be running. Still others mix and mingle, looking for the good word or tip that may pay off in a later race.

High Rollers

In the Matt Winn Room, where prominent businessmen and high rollers have enjoyed a private retreat for years, by invitation only, the atmosphere is one of librarylike serenity. Sipping their mint juleps, or more likely Scotch and sodas, executive types study the figures carefully before making their investments at special betting windows. Loud conversations or serious rooting for one's choice are considered bad form.

In the Skye Terrace dining rooms on the fourth, fifth, and sixth levels, a tapestry of prominent Americana celebrates the Derby in style. Waiters serve dinner and drinks throughout the afternoon, wagering windows and comfort facilities are right at hand, climate control makes the rooms comfortable no matter what the temperature outdoors, and the view of the track and the races from the broad balconies just outside is spectacular.

Countdown

With each race on the program, Derby Day tension builds, and it is thick enough to cut during the one-hour interval prior to the Run for the Roses. This unusually long preparation time is needed for the horses to be assembled and saddled in the handsome new paddock, for owners and their friends to wish one another good luck, and for thousands to view these colorful proceedings and return to their seats in time to join in the emotional singing of "My Old Kentucky Home" as the Derby entries walk onto the track. For many annual visitors to Churchill Downs, this moment is as wonderful to experience as the race itself.

They're Off!

The Derby telecast is usually scheduled from 5:00 to 6:00 P.M., with the Derby set for 5:40 P.M. There is no more electric moment in racing than when the announcer shouts, "They're off!" The crowd is watching history in the making. Those who limit their wagers to $2 are rooting just as hard as the plungers in the Skye Terrace who may have $5,000 or $10,000 or more on the horse of their choice. As the horses enter the stretch, the roar from the crowd seems to take on a life of its own. The race is over in about two minutes, but the 130,000 or so on hand—an average Derby crowd—have been through the wringer and are limp.

As the horses return amid thunderous applause to the unsaddling area in front of the stands and the winner is draped with the traditional blanket of red roses, the winning party is escorted from their box to the infield trophy presentation stand, where the governor of Kentucky and Churchill Downs president Tom Meeker are waiting to greet them. The Derby trophy, a loving cup of solid 14-karat gold, cost $5,000 for many years. When the price of gold started to rise in the 1970s, so did the cost of the trophy. An extra trophy is always kept in the track safe against the possibility of a dead heat. It hasn't happened yet, but the Churchill Downs people are ready if it does.

The winning party—owner, trainer, jockey, spouses, and friends—which may number fifty or more, is then escorted to the Directors' Lounge for a toast in traditional sterling silver julep goblets.

Owner, trainer, and jockey are spirited away for a brief interview session in the huge press box, where more than 1,000 journalists from all parts of the United States and many foreign countries have filed stories throughout Derby Week. Then the winners attend a reception at the Kentucky Derby Museum, crowded with notable celebrants who may watch the Derby again on videotape while toasting the victors.

The Purse

When Hoop Jr. won the 1945 Kentucky Derby for Fred Hooper of Miami, who had never owned a horse before, the purse to the winner was $64,850. The 1965 winner, Lucky Debonair, won $112,000 for the late Dan and Ada Rice of Chicago. Spend a Buck, whom Dennis Diaz of Tampa had bought for $12,500, won the 1985 Kentucky Derby and earned a winner's prize of $406,800.

Of course, the real value of a Kentucky Derby victory is not in the purse but in this classic's credentials for a horse's stud career. It has been estimated by bloodstock specialists that a Kentucky Derby winner can be syndicated after the victory for a price of at least $8 million to $10 million, depending upon his pedigree—and regardless of other victories that may come during the year. The winner also becomes the only horse eligible that year to win racing's most coveted prize, the Triple Crown, which has been won by only eleven horses in history.

A Winning Tradition

The Derby Winner's Party in the Directors' Lounge, overlooking the tulip garden, is slightly clamorous and fairly brief. In another era, when those participating were not eyeing their watches and rushing to the airport, the celebration had a more genteel quality.

When Colonel Matt Winn was president of Churchill Downs, and during the subsequent presidency of New York newspaperman Bill Corum, the owner of the Derby winner, his trainer, his rider, and a few guests were invited to Colonel Winn's apartment, a

Lord Derby, a special visitor in 1930

Victorian suite of rooms located just above the track's administrative offices. It was a charming residence overlooking a courtyard, with a long balcony the length of the suite.

A small jug band played for the guests, who gathered on the balcony in the twilight of a soft May evening and chatted quietly of the day's events, reconstructing every aspect of the victory. As the departing crowds passed through the courtyard below on their way to Central Avenue, they would turn and hail the winning party, who in turn would put down their mint juleps, Kentucky ham, and biscuits and wave back to the fans.

The celebration continued into the gathering darkness, and as the haunting blues of the jug band faded into the mild spring night, more than a few of the guests sat back in their chairs, sipped at their sour mash, and reflected that it doesn't get much better than this.

The humorist and philosopher Irvin S. Cobb, known as the Sage of Paducah, Kentucky, summed it up best when he said, "Until you've been to the Kentucky Derby, you ain't never been nowheres and you ain't never seen nothin'."

It's Derby time and at Derby time a man with a thimble has container enough to carry off all the common sense in Louisville.

Sports commentator Heywood Hale Broun once said, "The Kentucky Derby is a shared delusion. On the streets of Paris, Frenchmen stop their strolling. Drums beat in Africa, spelling out a message. Lamas will stop turning their prayer wheels, and successors to Chairman Mao will put down their chopsticks and ask, 'Who won the Kentucky Derby?' "

Two minutes in the running, the Derby involves Louisville every day of every year. By the late 1950s, the city recognized the Derby as more than a horse race. It was a piece of civic pride that touched not only Kentucky, but in fact reached out to the world as drawn by Broun. So the Derby Festival committee made the race the centerpiece of a weeklong carnival, a horsey Mardi Gras, complete with winged Pegasus parading down Main Street.

More than seventy events are designed as added attractions. Everyone, and everything, goes racing: marathoners, cyclists, balloonists—even paddle-wheelers on the Ohio. At Spalding College—in an event that is not part of the festival schedule—students dress rats in mock silks: "The Run for the Rodents."

Derby princesses. Blooming tulips. Bands marching in warm sunlight. It's springtime in the Bluegrass. And that's what the Derby is: spring's renewal. Whatever the calendar says is meaningless. Spring begins in Kentucky the same day every year. The first Saturday in May. Derby Day.

A concert with Kris Kristofferson. Revues with casts of hundreds. The Derby is no longer just a horse race, as the Super Bowl long ago quit being just a football game and the Indy 500 simply a contest for fast cars. Sports events now are civic celebrations. Churchill Downs estimates that the Derby's 1987 economic impact was around $200 million.

Everyone has the urge to race. Long-distance runners wind up at the Churchill Downs finish line. Waiters balance wine on trays in "The Run for the Rosé." And in "The Great Steamboat Race," the smaller Belle of Louisville *is the perennial underdog to Cincinnati's grand* Delta Queen. *If the Belle lacks steam power, it has cunning. It once won by sneaking passengers—the heaviest ones—onto the Queen to slow it down.*

The U.S. Air Force Thunderbirds overhead. A hot-air balloon up a tree. The nineteenth century coming around a bend. Louisville is a city alive in Derby Week. The horse race began when the train was opening up America. Now the race is as up-to-date as a jet fighter. What makes the Derby distinctive is Louisville's blending of the old and the new.

111

Horses raced on a downtown street in Louisville as early as 1783. But when the Woodlawn Course went bankrupt in 1870, the city was left without a racetrack. M. Lewis Clark, Jr., changed that five years later. On land three miles from the city—"a long buggy ride into the countryside," one man said—Clark built a new track. He called it the Louisville Jockey Club.

By 1883 the Jockey Club track was known as Churchill Downs, named for Clark's uncles John and Henry Churchill, who leased him the country land. A hundred years later, on the same land, the great racing domain is now part of the city.

Timeless beauty attaches to a racetrack. As they did at the Jockey Club a hundred years ago, men still spread water at Churchill Downs. And still they comb the dirt into shallow furrows.

The Derby was first the distance of a mile and a quarter in 1896, when the colt Ben Brush won in a time then listed as 2:07 3/4. Ninety years later, the timeless game had changed so little that on the same land, watered and harrowed as always, Ferdinand won the Derby in 2:02 4/5—less than five seconds faster than Ben Brush nearly a century earlier.

The mosaic of a racetrack is put together carefully, every piece just so. The starting gate has been pulled away, the track watered and harrowed. Now a man with a rake backs across the track. As he moves, he rakes away footprints. He does this not only to satisfy the artist's urge for a clean canvas. Footprints are incongruous shiny spots. Some horses shy from them—that is dangerous.

Twin spires. You know this can be only one racetrack in the world. The spires were raised at Churchill Downs in 1895 as part of an eleventh-hour effort to revitalize the failing track. With them came a new grandstand and, the following year, a new race length. The cornerstones of lasting success were put in place all at once.

Nightfall. Churchill Downs is ready for the dawn.

Caring for Champions

O n a foggy spring morning before World War I at Harry Payne Whitney's Brookdale Farm near Red Bank, New Jersey, James Rowe, Sr., who trained two Kentucky Derby winners, gave instructions to his celebrated exercise rider, Marshall Lilly.

"Go three-quarters and bring this colt back in 1:16," he said, and Lilly knew he didn't mean 1:16⅗.

Lilly, who always wore a black derby when he rode work, disappeared with the horse into the dense fog. When he rode back, Rowe showed his stopwatch to Lilly with the reading of 1:18.

"Sorry I messed up the work, Mr. Rowe," Lilly said, "but at the far turn, someone walked out on the track in front of me. Because of the fog, I didn't see him until it was too late."

"You should have rode him down," said Rowe gruffly.

"I did," Lilly said.

In those days of iron horses and iron men, James Rowe, Sr., was tough on those he trained and those who served him. America's leading jockey from 1871 through 1873, he later retired to become a trainer.

Rowe's Roses

His greatest horse, Hindoo, bred in Kentucky by Daniel Swigert, was by Virgil out of Florence. The talented colt won seven of nine starts at 2. Under Rowe's expert supervision, Hindoo at 3 had one of the finest seasons of any horse in the nineteenth century, winning eighteen of twenty starts, including the seventh Kentucky Derby in 1881 by four lengths.

In 1914 one of the best 2-year-olds at Brookdale Farm was a lovely filly by Broomstick out of Jersey Lightning. Whitney called her Regret. Trained by Rowe that August, Regret won all three of her starts against colts at Saratoga, and in rousing fashion.

After wintering in New Jersey, Regret was trained for the Kentucky Derby as her first race of 1915. Rowe, assisted by Marshall Lilly, went about his preparation with typical thoroughness and care. Sent to Louisville about two weeks prior to the Derby, Regret did not travel well, however, and was off her feed upon arrival. Her first work at Churchill Downs, over the Derby distance of a mile and a quarter, was accomplished in a pedestrian 2:14⅗. But then, three days before the race, she came back with another mile and a quarter in 2:08⅗. The public never had any doubts. Regret was the solid choice at 5–2 in a field of sixteen, the largest field in some forty years of Derby history. With Joe Notter in the irons, Regret went to the front at the start and remained in the lead all the way, winning by two lengths. Regret, the first filly to win the Kentucky Derby, was the talk of the country.

Derby Dick Thompson

Before the era of Plain Ben Jones, no trainer in America had more of an impact on the Derby than Herbert John "Derby Dick" Thompson— winner of four Kentucky Derbys for Colonel Edward Riley Bradley of Idle Hour Stock Farm between 1921 and 1933.

In 1921 Thompson ran two of Bradley's colts in the 47th Kentucky Derby. One was Black Servant, a favorite of the Colonel's. The other colt, Behave Yourself, had been a moderate 2-year-old. The Colonel, a gambler who enjoyed having an opinion backed by cash whenever his horses raced, wagered heavily on Black Servant in the future book.

Under Lucien Lyke, the speedy Black Servant set the pace in the Derby. Behave Yourself raced eighth in the field of twelve under Charlie Thompson but gained ground and was dead even with Black Servant at the eighth pole. It was not until the final stride that the winner was known— Behave Yourself, by a head.

Colonel Bradley smiled as he received the trophy

and a check for $38,450; however, it was reported later that the victory had cost him as much—or more—in his losing bets.

Thompson's second Derby victory came in 1926 when he again had two good colts for Colonel Bradley. Bubbling Over, regarded as the better, had been a top 2-year-old, with seven victories from ten starts. The other Idle Hour colt was Bagenbaggage, who had tired to finish eighth in the Preakness five days earlier (in those years the Preakness preceded the Derby).

In the 52nd Kentucky Derby, Bubbling Over, with Albert Johnson aboard, went right to the front and remained there, winning by five lengths over Bagenbaggage, who finished second.

Colonel Bradley's Burgoo King (by Bubbling Over) was an easy winner of the 58th Kentucky Derby in 1932. Always close to the pace-setting Economic, who finished second, Burgoo King accelerated in the upper stretch under Eugene James and went on to win by five lengths at odds of 11–2.

The Fighting Finish

Thompson's fourth and most celebrated Derby victory came the following year, in 1933, under bizarre circumstances. Going into the Derby, Colonel Bradley's Brokers Tip (by Black Toney) had never won a race. Don Meade was in the irons on that fateful May 6, and so far back after the start that Brokers Tip appeared to have little chance. But the colt gained momentum and moved into second position in the stretch.

Head Play, with Herb Fisher aboard, had the lead, but when he passed the furlong pole, Brokers Tip was almost abreast on the inside. The two horses dueled through the final furlong with Fisher reaching for Meade's saddlecloth and Meade grabbing for Fisher's boot. This battle continued almost to the wire, and Brokers Tip was the winner by a nose.

That Derby was to be the only race Brokers Tip ever won in fourteen attempts, and ironically, it was also to be the last Derby triumph for Dick

Thompson and Colonel Bradley. Thompson was hailed as a great trainer and a great gentleman who not once during his long career was ever punished, reprimanded, or even questioned by stewards.

Colonel Bradley delivered his own epitaph before a congressional committee inquiring into a crime. "I've been a gambler all my life," he said, "and I've always paid off one hundred cents on the dollar."

Sunny Jim

On the rainy afternoon of June 15, 1963, a crippled old man walked onto the racetrack at Aqueduct after the fourth race, and the moment he was spotted by the crowd, a roaring ovation filled the air and lasted for many minutes.

It was retirement day for James Edward Fitzsimmons—"Sunny Jim" to the racing world—and he was stepping down a month before his eighty-ninth birthday. He had his last winner, King's Story, in the Miss Woodford Stakes at Monmouth Park that afternoon. King's Story was his 2,330th winner and his 149th stakes winner, of which three were Kentucky Derby victories. His horses earned more than $13 million.

There has never been a horse trainer on the American turf more revered than Mr. Fitz, not only for his remarkable record and the success he enjoyed with such cracks as Gallant Fox, Omaha, Nashua, and Bold Ruler, but also for his personality and cheerful disposition.

Fitzsimmons had only a few strong convictions. One of them was that the owners were the most important people in racing because they put up their money and put on the show. Another was that horses should be fit when they ran.

Two Triple Crowns

In 1930 Fitzsimmons arrived at Churchill Downs with the solid favorite, Gallant Fox. The Belair Stud colt, owned and bred by William Woodward, Sr., chairman of the Jockey Club, was a promising 2-year-old who developed into a great 3-year-old. A

The Fighting Finish, 1933 Derby

son of Sir Gallahad III, Gallant Fox won the Wood Memorial and then the Preakness on May 9. Eight days later, on May 17, he captured the 56th Kentucky Derby by two convincing lengths under Earl Sande. The Fox of Belair took the lead on the backstretch and never looked back. He then captured the Belmont Stakes for a sweep of the Triple Crown.

Mr. Fitz returned to Churchill Downs in 1935 with Omaha, son of Gallant Fox. Omaha had been a fair 2-year-old, but he had come to hand quickly that spring and was third in the Wood Memorial. With William "Smokey" Saunders in the irons, Omaha started that 61st Kentucky Derby far back in a field of eighteen. The colt then moved to the outside and was in front before the quarter-pole, holding Roman Soldier safe to score by a length and a half.

One week later, Omaha won the Preakness, then completed a sweep of the Triple Crown in the Belmont, becoming the only son of a Triple Crown winner to win the Triple Crown himself.

Sunny Jim and Belair Stud had their third Kentucky Derby triumph in 1939 when Johnstown (by Jamestown) won by eight lengths as the 3–5 favorite. Jimmy Stout, who had been unseated from Granville in the Derby three years earlier, was pleased to ride Johnstown to victory.

Sunny Jim enjoyed much of his greatest success during his eighties, but when his legs no longer could carry him on his morning rounds, he retired. He died in Miami on March 11, 1966, sunny and alert to the end.

Hirsch's Bold Ventures

Like Sunny Jim, Max Hirsch also trained three Kentucky Derby winners and was one of a kind. A brilliant horseman during a career that covered almost seventy years, he was possessed of a gruff voice and manner that masked a gregarious nature. Again like Fitzsimmons, Hirsch began his career as a jockey, but soon stopped riding to become a trainer. He was a natural, and quickly attracted notice with his many successes.

In 1936 Hirsch saddled Morton Schwartz's Bold Venture (by St. Germans) to win the 62nd Kentucky Derby with young Ira Hanford in the saddle. Bold Venture, a moderately successful 2-year-old, was trained to the minute for the Derby—but he needed a bit of luck to win. Brevity, the 4–5 favorite, had an unsteady trip, and Granville, another good prospect, lost his rider at the start of the race.

When Robert Kleberg, Jr., head of the million-acre King Ranch, came into racing, Max Hirsch purchased Bold Venture as a stallion for him. Bold Venture later became the sire of King Ranch's two Derby winners, Assault and Middleground. Assault, troubled throughout his career by a club foot, won the Wood Memorial at 3 but was still a moderate prospect for the 72nd Run for the Roses in 1946. With Warren Mehrtens up, Assault came from off the pace on a slow track to win by eight lengths. He then went on to complete a sweep of the Triple Crown and become Horse of the Year.

Four years later, Hirsch turned in another outstanding training achievement with Middleground. A winner of four of five starts at 2, Middleground, who was ridden by young Bill Boland, was 8–1 for the 76th Kentucky Derby in 1950. Always well placed, Middleground moved up to the front in the stretch and then held off Hill Prince, the Wood Memorial winner ridden by Eddie Arcaro, to score by a length and a quarter in a lively 2:01⅗, for Hirsch's final Derby win.

Hirsch was as renowned for his hospitality as for his skill as a trainer. Racing men came to him for advice on various matters, and he was as generous with his time and keen judgment as he was with his food. He barked his "good mornings" like a wounded grizzly, but a twinkle in his eye and a smile he could not hide revealed the real Max Hirsch.

Luro's Luck

Along with the Jones boys, Horatio Luro ranks high among the best of the Derby trainers. Celebrated for his debonair manner, he was put to the test on

Colonel E.R. Bradley and "Derby Dick" Thompson

September 17, 1956. A 3-year-old filly named Nautigal had a four-length lead at midstretch in a grass race at the Atlantic City Race Course. She looked like a certain winner, when suddenly, she made a sharp left-hand turn. Bolting through the hedge that served as the inner rail, she plunged into the shallow infield lake, struggled as she became entrapped in the muddy bottom, and soon tired and fell to her knees. She drowned in two feet of water. When the state veterinarian pronounced her dead, Luro was in shock. In the "axsent" that has become so familiar and so dear to racing men around the world, he asked, "How do I call the owner tonight and tell him his horse was leading in the stretch and then drowned?"

Very few situations involving horses have stumped Horatio Luro since he came to the United States from his native Argentina in the mid-1930s. He saddled Kentucky Derby winners Decidedly (1962) and Northern Dancer (1964), both of whom set track records at Churchill Downs. Northern Dancer later became one of the world's most influential stallions, as did another of Luro's racing stars of the 1940s, Princequillo. He also trained such cracks as Talon, Rico Monte, and many more.

Five years after Luro's Atlantic City mishap, George Pope, the steamship-company heir, sent him a gray 2-year-old colt by the 1954 Kentucky Derby winner, Determine, himself a gray. The homebred Decidedly bloomed for the patient Luro in the spring. With Bill Hartack as his rider, he finished strongly to be second in Keeneland's Blue Grass Stakes and came to the 88th Kentucky Derby of 1962 in peak form.

It was a Derby full of speed, and Luro's instructions to Hartack were brief: Keep him well off the pace and then bring him on for a strong finish. As Ridan, Admiral's Voyage, and Sunrise County destroyed one another near the lead, Hartack sat patiently. He moved with Decidedly on the turn, was a close third at the eighth pole, and came on to win by a conclusive 2¼ lengths. The time was 2:00⅖—a Derby record. Until 1964 . . .

The Dancer from Canada

Luro had trained horses, including the talented Nearctic and Natalma, for the Canadian industrialist E.P. Taylor. When these two were bred, they produced a husky but smallish bay colt with three white stockings who failed to bring a reserve price of $25,000 at Taylor's 1962 annual yearling sale. Taylor kept the colt and named him Northern Dancer.

Sent to Luro, Northern Dancer proved a first-class 2-year-old, winning seven of nine starts, including Aqueduct's prestigious Remsen Stakes. Late that fall, however, he developed a quarter crack, and manager Joe Thomas planned to bring him back to the farm for a long rest. Luro suggested an alternative step, to bind the crack with a vulcanized rubber process known as the bane patch.

With only a minimum loss of time, Northern Dancer resumed training, won the Flamingo Stakes and Florida Derby, and then bid for the 90th Kentucky Derby on May 2, 1964. With Hartack up, the Dancer from Canada was second choice to George Pope's Hill Rise, the Santa Anita Derby winner.

Escaping a trap along the backstretch, Hartack got Northern Dancer into high gear relatively early, sent him to the lead near the quarter-pole, and then held off the late charge of the huge Hill Rise to score by a neck in the new record time of 2:00. The good little horse had beaten the good big horse in a classic struggle.

Luro's Law

Having retired from training at eighty-three, Luro is still active as an owner, breeder, bloodstock dealer, and consultant to prominent stables. His great skill in harnessing Northern Dancer's prodigious speed to stay the classic distances is legend in the industry, and Luro's Law, pertaining to the conservation of racing stock, has become Gospel. In the words of El Gran Señor: "Do not squeeze the lemon dry."

Like Son, Like Father

In most instances, a son follows in a father's footsteps. In the case of Lucien Laurin, who saddled Riva Ridge (1972) and Secretariat (1973) to win consecutive Kentucky Derbys, the situation was reversed. When his son Roger, an accomplished trainer, vacated the job at Meadow Stable, Lucien filled it.

Mind you, Lucien Laurin was already a successful trainer in his own right. As Roger left, he commented to his father that there was a very good 2-year-old prospect in the barn. By First Landing out of Iberia, he was named Riva Ridge.

Riva Ridge had natural speed, winning seven of nine starts in 1971 to become 2-year-old champion. Winter book favorite for the 1972 Kentucky Derby, the colt developed physically and was a clever winner of the Blue Grass Stakes at Keeneland that spring. He was favored at 3–2 in the 98th running of the Derby and won it under Ron Turcotte by almost four lengths.

A National Treasure

Just as Riva Ridge was concluding his Triple Crown campaign, another Meadow Stable horse with spectacular bloodlines came onto the national scene. He was by the champion sire Bold Ruler out of the good producer Somethingroyal, and he was called Secretariat.

As a 2-year-old Secretariat won seven of nine starts and was named Horse of the Year, the first juvenile to win that honor. As he turned 3, he was syndicated by Seth Hancock of Claiborne Farm for a record $6,080,000, based on thirty-two shares at $190,000 each.

A standout choice for the spring classics of 1973, Secretariat dominated his very first race as a 3-year-old, winning Aqueduct's Bay Shore Stakes by more than four lengths on March 17. Then, on April 7, he electrified New Yorkers by racing a mile in 1:33⅖ to win the Gotham Stakes by three lengths at 1–10. Some spoke of him as the "Big Train." The Wood Memorial at Aqueduct on April 21 was to be the final ceremony before the coronation in the Kentucky Derby, but the Big Train was derailed, finishing a weak third.

The ensuing two weeks were the worst of Laurin's life. As all of America offered theories about Secretariat's loss, Laurin was under siege by the colt's owners. Heated discussions, some in public, had Laurin ashen-faced and trembling by Derby Day.

Secretariat trained smartly at Churchill Downs and made a splendid appearance under jockey Ron Turcotte for the 99th Derby on May 5. Leaving the far turn, Turcotte got into Secretariat with his whip and the Red Horse responded. He moved into second position approaching the quarter-pole, then felt the whip again as he took command. Through the stretch, the cheers of the large crowd rose in intensity as Secretariat drew off to win by 2½ lengths. Another roar followed when it was announced that Secretariat's mile and a quarter in 1:59⅖ was a new track record.

A vindicated Laurin shipped Secretariat to Baltimore for the Preakness, which he won comfortably by 2½ lengths. Secretariat saved his finest hour for the Belmont Stakes on June 9, winning by thirty-one lengths, fracturing the old mark of 2:26⅗ with a scintillating twelve furlongs in 2:24, a world record. He had become racing's first Triple Crown winner in twenty-five years.

Woody's Derbys

Almost every trainer in America wanted to win the 100th Derby on May 4, 1974. The honor of honors fell to a hardboot's hardboot from Kentucky, Woodford Cefis "Woody" Stephens, who collaborated with John Olin's Cannonade and Angel Cordero, Jr., for a stirring victory.

That was the first of two Kentucky Derby triumphs for Stephens—Swale was the other in 1984—and it is safe to say that both were unforgettable, for different reasons. But then the unforgettable has been the norm for Stephens, who in over four decades as a trainer has saddled more stakes

Horatio A. Luro

winners than any other horseman in the East.

Having grown up in the heart of horse country, Stephens made horses his life's work early on. At thirteen, he broke yearlings, and at fifteen left high school to take a job as an exercise rider, which led to a career as a jockey. On opening day in 1931 at Hialeah at age eighteen, Stephens rode his first winner. Eventually gaining too much weight to ride, he first groomed horses and then took jobs as an assistant and then as a head trainer. He came to New York in 1945, and in 1957 began a long and successful association with the Cain Hoy stable of Captain Harry Guggenheim. In 1973 when Olin sent Cannonade to Stephens to train, Stephens was running a successful public stable.

The largest field in Kentucky Derby history—twenty-three starters—turned out for the centennial running. Stephens's entry of Cannonade and his stablemate, Judger, was favored at 3–2, with Laffit Pincay, Jr., on Judger and Cordero on Cannonade. The huge field self-destructed, horses bumping one another right and left. Judger was squeezed at the start and lost position, then had a rough trip the rest of the way, finishing eighth. The only horse to have a successful journey was Cannonade. Cordero, bright and innovative, guided the colt between and around horses and prevailed by 2¼ lengths, finishing the ten panels in 2:04.

Triple Crown Tragedy

Stephens was to gain his second Kentucky Derby victory ten years later with Claiborne Farm's Swale. Swale won the Belmont Stakes but dropped dead a week later after an easy gallop. Stephens was deeply affected by the loss but rebounded to an unprecedented string of five victories in the Belmont, a record likely to stand the test of time.

Like Father, Like Son

One of the finest Kentucky Derby records of our time belongs to LeRoy Jolley, who won America's premier race with Foolish Pleasure (1975) and the

filly Genuine Risk (1980), finished second with Honest Pleasure (1976) and General Assembly (1979), and was third with Ridan (1962), all well before his forty-fifth birthday.

Son of the outstanding horseman Moody Jolley, LeRoy Jolley developed a style of his own and is the epitome of the modern trainer: closely tuned in to racing throughout the world, bright, articulate, and highly mobile.

In 1973 Moody Jolley was attracted at the yearling sales by a colt by the Bold Ruler stallion What a Pleasure out of a Tom Fool mare, Fool-Me-Not. The yearling toed out rather noticeably, but Moody Jolley thought the problem was not insurmountable and acquired him for $20,000 for John L. Greer. Foolish Pleasure won all seven of his starts at 2 and was the future-book favorite for the 101st Kentucky Derby of 1975. He did nothing to harm his stature by accounting for Hialeah's Flamingo Stakes and Aqueduct's Wood Memorial at 3, and he shipped to Churchill Downs as a solid 2–1 favorite to win the roses.

In a gesture of confidence in his son, Moody Jolley remained at home during Derby Week, permitting the full spotlight of publicity to focus on the thirty-seven-year-old LeRoy Jolley, a seasoned trainer. Bombay Duck set the pace in the Derby with Foolish Pleasure well back in a field of fifteen. Beautifully mannered, Foolish Pleasure could be placed anywhere by jockey Jacinto Vasquez, who followed Jolley's orders and refrained from contesting the early pace. In the stretch Foolish Pleasure, on the outside, sailed past the embattled leaders to win by 1¾ lengths.

Genuine Risk

Mr. and Mrs. Bert Firestone's son, Matthew, a keen racing fan, accompanied his parents to the yearling sales in 1978 and urged them to pay attention to a filly by Exclusive Native who caught his eye. They were able to land her for $32,000, and, trained by LeRoy Jolley, she proved a good one from the outset. Genuine Risk won all four of her starts at 2,

The grandstand c.1905

and both Firestone and LeRoy Jolley began to think of her in terms of the Kentucky Derby. No filly had won the Derby since Regret in 1915, and few had even run in it.

Jolley trained Genuine Risk very lightly that winter, not starting her until March 19 at Gulfstream Park, when she beat other fillies. She then shipped to New York for a one-mile filly race on April 5, which she won. That set the stage for a race against colts in the Wood Memorial on April 19. Genuine Risk, under Jacinto Vasquez, was mildly regarded at 8–1. Racing a consistent third throughout the nine furlongs, the filly finished in that position, convincing the majority that she was not a good risk against colts. Genuine Risk went off at 13–1 for the 106th Kentucky Derby on May 3, 1980.

As he had done with Foolish Pleasure, Vasquez sat chilly, well off the early pace set by Plugged Nickle and Rockhill Native. The filly took the lead entering the stretch as the crowd roared its approval; quickly opening a one-length advantage, she then continued on to beat the stretch-running Rumbo by a length. As was the case with Regret sixty-five years earlier, Genuine Risk's Derby triumph aroused great national interest in racing. Finishing second in the Preakness and in the Belmont, she became the first filly to run in all of the Triple Crown events.

The Two-Minute Lick

In the long history of the Kentucky Derby, few trainers mystified newsmen more with the style and substance of their preparation than Cuban-born Lazaro Sosa Barrera did as he prepared Bold Forbes, owned by Enrique Rodriguez Tizol, for the 102nd Run for the Roses on May 1, 1976.

Barrera was faced with a problem, which he handled in brilliant fashion. Bold Forbes was born with great natural speed, and in the first seven starts of his career, he was always in front in his races. The problem was to condition Bold Forbes to carry that speed for a mile and a quarter. It was a formidable assignment, particularly because his chief rival, Honest Pleasure, was full of speed, too.

Barrera's tool was the two-minute lick. Instead of the usual workout of six furlongs or a mile, the trainer had Bold Forbes gallop every day for a mile and a half to two miles, with every furlong in a slow :15, picking up the tempo toward the finish. As Bold Forbes went around, reporters, wondering if the colt had a physical problem, asked Barrera when his horse was going to work. Only the observant realized that Barrera was succeeding with his project.

So that Honest Pleasure's speed would not give him an edge, Barrera instructed Bold Forbes's jockey, Angel Cordero, Jr., to try to get out of the gate first to control the pace. Breaking from post 2 to Honest Pleasure's post 5, Cordero was able to gain an immediate lead, which he held the rest of the way around. Every time Braulio Baeza, on Honest Pleasure, tried to pass Bold Forbes, Cordero let out another notch. Bold Forbes won by a length, the Derby timed in 2:01⅗.

The Battle of the Giants

In 1977 Louis Wolfson, master of Harbor View Farm, sent Barrera his 2-year-old colt by Exclusive Native out of Won't Tell You by Crafty Admiral. His name was Affirmed.

Affirmed, who won his first start at Belmont Park that spring, met Calumet Farm's Alydar in his second appearance, on June 15, and beat him by five lengths. It was the beginning of the greatest rivalry in the history of thoroughbred racing. They met again five times that year, with Affirmed beating Alydar three times and Alydar beating Affirmed twice.

The next spring Affirmed won two stakes races in California. Meanwhile, Alydar captured the Flamingo at Hialeah and the Florida Derby. For their final tune-ups, Affirmed won the nine-furlong Hollywood Derby while Alydar scored a thirteen-length victory in the Blue Grass Stakes. The immovable object and the irresistible force were on schedule toward an epic meeting in Louisville.

No two-minute licks for Affirmed in his preparation at Churchill Downs. Laz sent him a mile and an eighth in 1:56⅕ during the weekend prior to the Derby and then came back, three days before the race, with a crisp five panels in :59. Alydar, in contrast, had only a half-mile in :50 during the nine-day period between the Blue Grass and the Derby.

The Battle of the Giants, attracting the third-largest Derby crowd up to that time, saw Steve Cauthen on Affirmed open a two-length advantage at the eighth pole; Alydar under Jorge Velasquez was running third. It became obvious Alydar was not going to make it, but the big chestnut colt drove to within 1½ lengths of Affirmed in the final strides. Still, it was a brilliant victory for Affirmed, who ran his ten panels in 2:01⅕.

The rivals were to meet again in the Preakness on May 20, with Affirmed the winner by a desperate neck this time. They were eyeball-to-eyeball in most of the stretch run as a record crowd went wild with excitement.

The Belmont Stakes on June 10 attracted 65,417, who favored Affirmed at 3–5 over Alydar at 11–10. Through the final mile they were head-and-head. Alydar appeared to inch forward briefly. In the stretch, however, Affirmed was a bulldog, prevailing by a head in one of the greatest races in American classic history. In winning the Triple Crown, Affirmed had a combined margin over Alydar of less than two lengths.

One year after his triumph, Lazaro Barrera, of Marianao, Cuba; Mexico City; New York; Los Angeles; and a hundred different cities in between, was elected to the Racing Hall of Fame in Saratoga Springs, New York. He took his rightful place with the best of the best.

Comes the dawn softly. Mist rises from tubs of warm water. Birds in green trees begin their gentle music. Horses take in air, back from a gallop. The chill of the morning touches the warm vapors off a working horse's shoulder and steam rises a foot high, the horse now moving in a misty aura.

They are athletes. Sometimes we forget. We think of them as something else. But what? Black Beauty? A carousel pony? As surely as O.J. Simpson was born to run, so were these horses. And as surely as O.J. worked at his gift, so did Secretariat. Comes the dawn softly, and the Secretariats are out there, working.

Come now, at dawn, to the barns at Churchill Downs. Grooms carry the tubs, now emptied. They have bathed the big horses. They move in the mist of their own making into the barn, past an old Kentucky hardboot, a trainer. He leans against his barn, the sunlight soft on his tan felt hat.

The sounds of the morning: birds awakening, a cat's meow, boot heels crunching tanbark, the falling of hooves against the dirt. Such a sound is a horse at work— the sound swelling as the horse comes toward you, growing full and frightening, then fading, the horse past you, the drumming rhythm a memory.

"One more night of no sleepin', I'll be sleepin' standin' up durin' the Derby," a trainer mutters. This is his place, a barn. The smells are his, leather and liniment, straw and manure.

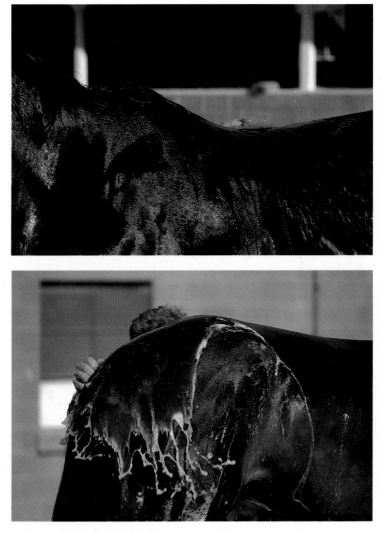

Because they are athletes,
racehorses are pampered by
a crew whose job it is to see
to it that they come to work
at the top of their game. This
pampering keeps a groom on
call twenty-four hours a
day. Not that Shotgun Foley
minded. He was a groom
all his life. He believed horses
are smarter than people.
They don't get drunk. They
don't ask questions. " 'Sway
it oughta be. To each his
own."

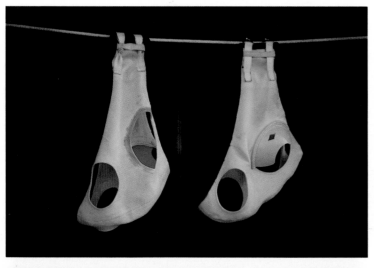

The tools of a groom's trade. Blinkers. Leg wraps. Saddles well worn. All at the barn. If the texture of life is suggested by detail, what should we make of a horseman who hangs wraps from pins on a rope? And what about the man who just drapes the wraps over the line? Is the first man careful? Or is the draper more efficient? Or maybe he just lost his pins.

Shotgun Foley, a groom for most of his sixty years, said in 1966 that his Derby horse Advocator needed only a few special things. "Carrots, mostly."

Shotgun carried nine safety pins clipped to his pants leg. "I hook the leg wraps with these pins."

"I've been getting up before 5:30 for over forty years now." Shotgun Foley hadn't shaved for two weeks. No need to. A man on a racetrack just needs to hang the leg wraps, dry the blinkers, keep house. "First thing I do is check the horse. Then I get out the feed box. After the horse works, I clean him up and rub him down."

Shotgun Foley's cap looked older than he did, and he looked to be a million. Age didn't bother him, " 'cause the horse don't care how old you are. All he cares about is gettin' his oats. Don't give him his oats, you mightn't get any older." Old Shotgun figured he'd cleaned up and rubbed down a thousand horses. "Only thing I never did was ride one. It mighta been fun."

The tools of Shotgun's trade hang to dry at the barn. It's late morning. The day's heavy work is done.

In '66 Advocator finished second in the Derby, and Shotgun, as part of the athlete's team, was pleased to say, "I love that horse. And you know why? 'Cause I got down on that horse. Bet my week's pay. And right now, I got me some green presidents in my pants pocket."

Leg wraps, or bandages, help protect a horse from cutting himself while running or walking. Under the wrapping is a layer of soft, cottony cloth—a cushion against the stray hoof that might slice the horse's leg.

Cooling water run on a hot horse's legs brings relief after a workout, just as an ice bag on a pitcher's arm soothes when his work is done.

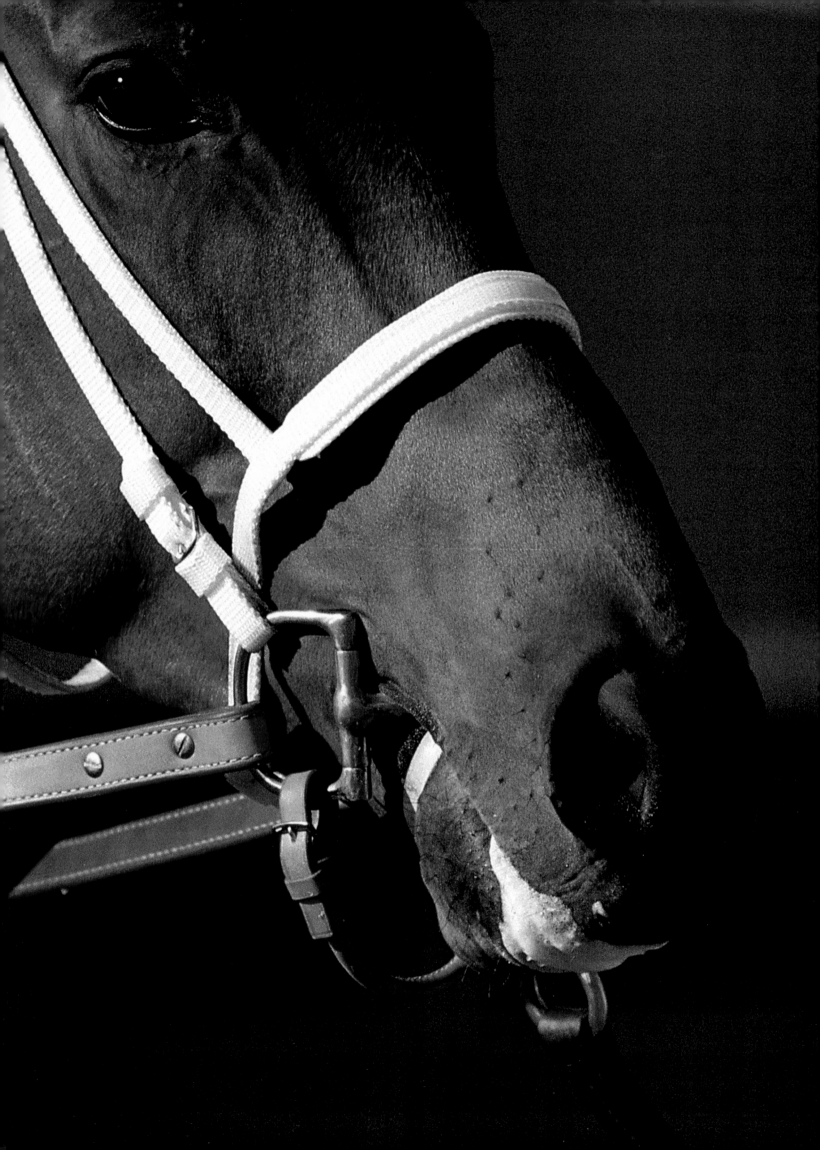

They've worked through the morning, worked until lather comes onto their bridles. Hot-walkers take them now. They'll walk the shed row until they've cooled out.

If you talk to a hot-walker, you hear a racetracker's story. All fascinating, some of it may even be true, though truth is held in such high regard that race folks generally reserve it for use when a jail sentence gets in the conversation.

Take Tommy (Long) Crawford. Back from walking a "hot" in Derby Week of '87, he said, "They call me Tommy Long 'cause I was long, tall, and skinny. Used to, I could boot and scoot." Tommy Long could ride, he meant. Said he also pitched for a black baseball team that went to Cuba in the twenties.

Tommy Long made a quarter to work out horses back then. Now they pay him $186 a week to work in the barns. Too bad, he said, he came along before Jackie Robinson, or he could have played big-league ball.

He played center field once in the White Sox park in Chicago. "You shoulda seen what happened. A boy hit a ball goin' outta the park. I was watchin' it go clean outta the park—when it hit a pigeon. Killed the pigeon. And I caught the ball in one hand. And I caught the pigeon in the other hand."

Tommy Long stood in the warm morning sun, a smile this big. He reached high to make those catches one more time.

With his smith's tongs, the farrier extracts nails from a hoof, removing a shoe in preparation to fit a new one. A horse's shoes are checked daily, but he normally needs a new set only once a month. Horseshoes once were steel forged in the smithy's fire, but now the racers wear aluminum, which is lighter and cheaper. "A blacksmith never gets his hands dirty anymore," said Pat Hillock, who shod fifteen Derby winners in a fifty-year career.

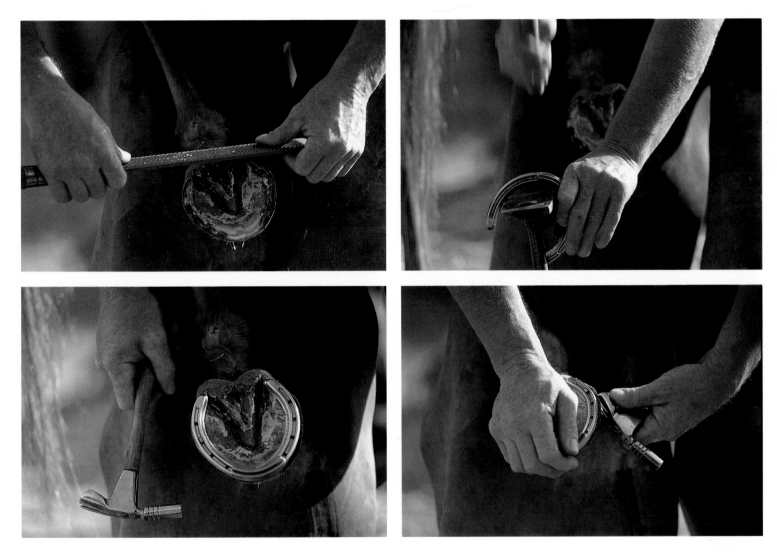

With the old shoe off, the farrier uses a rasp to level the hoof's bottom. The hoof is the equivalent of a human fingernail—it grows and needs to be trimmed. When preparing the new shoe, the farrier often must hammer it into a shape to fit the horse.

Done with the nailing, the farrier trims the hoof's edge to a clean line.

From trainers to grooms to farriers, the thoroughbred's handlers have brought the runner to race day at the peak of physical condition. Exercise riders have worked the athlete in situations designed to identify his strengths and weaknesses.

It has been long, hard work with no promise of reward. In fact, the odds say you'll fail many more times than you'll succeed.

It's time to go racing. It's time for the pony riders to get dressed up for the party. Each runner goes to the post accompanied by a lead pony. And it's traditional at Derby time for the ponies to be decked out in their finest livery. So it's time to braid their manes and tails. It's time to attach a flower or two to the bridle. It's time for the Kentucky Derby.

Big Little Men

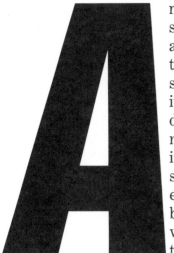America's sporting scene is stacked against the small athlete, and even when there is a division for him, such as lightweight boxing, it is the heavyweight divisions that are in the national spotlight. Not so in racing. Here, *only* the small, light athlete may experience the thrill of being a jockey, may know what it is to crouch low on the neck of a 1,000-pound thoroughbred moving like the wind, to dream of winning the Kentucky Derby.

Making the Weight

To be a jockey, a rider should ideally weigh from 108 to 114 pounds. Although the colts in the Derby all carry 126 pounds (fillies carry 121 pounds), other races throughout the year may require horses to carry 112 pounds or less. Naturally this greatly reduces a heavier jockey's opportunities for rides. To ensure that all horses are carrying the exact weight required, before each race the jockeys are weighed out holding their saddles. One-pound slabs of lead are added into special pockets in the saddlepad until the total combined weight of jockey and saddle is correct. Ideally, trainers prefer a jockey to weigh close to the amount required; one of the axioms of the sport is that live weight—the jockey—is better than dead weight—lead in the saddle—because live weight shifts with the horse.

The Ordeal of Dieting

Although many trainers will allow a horse to carry a pound or two over the required weight to get a particularly skilled jockey, most stay away from the "mucksacks," as perennially overweight jockeys are sometimes called. Not only do racing rules prohibit a horse from running with more than five pounds over the required weight, but the heavy jockey, who must continually reduce, is apt to be weak from the effort.

For many jockeys, making the weight is a constant ordeal. They eat little, stay on strict diets, and endure the tortures of sitting in a sweat box to reduce water weight before a race.

In past eras, when jockeys did not know about proper nutrition, severe dieting often shortened their lives. The most famous example was the brilliant black jockey Isaac Murphy, whose percentage of winners—44 percent—is still the record ninety-two years after his premature death at the age of thirty-five. The winner of three Kentucky Derbys in the late nineteenth century, the five-foot-tall Murphy was troubled by weight throughout his career. During the long off-season he would balloon up to 140 pounds and then would have to fight hard to get down to 105 pounds, his regular riding weight.

On one occasion, in 1895, his final season of riding, Murphy had the mount on the fine racemare Firenzi in the Monmouth Handicap at old Monmouth Park. Despite carrying topweight of 128 pounds, Firenzi was the 6–5 favorite to beat colts. However, she finished out of the money, and there was criticism of Murphy's performance. Some thought he was drunk. He later said that during the race he had suffered an attack of dizziness so severe that it was a miracle he had been able to remain on the horse to the finish.

Racing's Earl Sande—immortalized in Damon Runyon's poetry as "The Handy Guy"—had similar difficulty with weight, suffering stomach troubles throughout his career. His weight problem prompted him to "retire" three times. For his last comeback in 1953—at the age of fifty-five—he reduced from 140 to 113 pounds, an effort that was to take its toll. His health deteriorated gradually, and fifteen years later he was dead.

Many top trainers, in fact, have been jockeys who became too heavy to ride. Among these are winning Derby trainers James Rowe, Sr. (Hindoo, 1881; Regret, 1915); Sunny Jim Fitzsimmons

(Gallant Fox, 1930; Omaha, 1935; Johnstown, 1939); Lucien Laurin (Riva Ridge, 1972; Secretariat, 1973); and Woody Stephens (Cannonade, 1974; Swale, 1984). The only man ever to earn the distinction of both riding *and* training a Derby winner was Johnny Longden. Twenty-six years after riding Count Fleet to win the Triple Crown, Longden returned to Louisville in 1969 as a trainer to bring home the roses with Frank McMahon's Majestic Prince.

Bug-Boys

In contrast to "mucksacks," apprentice jockeys are generally underweight. To encourage trainers to use them, apprentices are given a weight allowance of five to ten pounds, except in handicaps and stakes. This status is indicated in the race program by a buglike asterisk beside the jockey's name, hence the name "bug-boy." Three asterisks indicate a jockey who has not yet won five races—a "triple-bug," who gets the greatest weight allowance of ten pounds. The apprentice period usually lasts a year from the date of the jockey's fifth win. The weight allowance does seem to make a difference, and many top apprentices fade from the scene once they lose this advantage.

Top jockeys usually show their brilliance early. Among the most renowned who went on to excel is Steve Cauthen, America's leading apprentice in 1976. Two years later the eighteen-year-old Cauthen rode Harbor View Farm's Affirmed to win the Triple Crown over Alydar in one of racing's most famous rivalries. Cauthen now rides in England, where he has led the winning jockeys' list three times.

In the 1950 Derby, sixteen-year-old apprentice Bill Boland was so intimidated by trainer Max Hirsch that he scored a victory with Middleground over Eddie Arcaro on the highly regarded Hill Prince that a more experienced rider might have missed. "Max Hirsch trained Middleground and warned Boland not to move a muscle until midstretch," Arcaro recalled. "I don't think any other rider would have waited as long as Boland did, but the kid was scared to death of the Old Man, so he waited till the eighth pole and then accelerated to win it. I just couldn't catch him with Hill Prince, who was the better horse. He beat Middleground by five lengths in the Preakness."

A less successful story is that of Ronnie Franklin, who had the great fortune to get the mount on the 1979 Kentucky Derby and Preakness winner, Spectacular Bid. In the Belmont, however, Franklin's inexperience, a safety pin, and a misjudged workout cost Bid the Triple Crown. The colt had a severe workout on an off track early in Belmont Week, which took a lot out of him. He then stepped on a safety pin the morning of the Belmont, injuring his foot. In the race itself Franklin ran him too hard on the lead, squandering his reserve. Bid could finish no better than third, and Franklin was never to ride him again. That the brilliant gray colt "should" have won the Triple Crown that year is widely accepted. He retired the following year with a sensational twenty-six wins, two seconds, and one third in thirty starts and earnings of $2,781,608, then a record for a horse. In fact, Spectacular Bid so intimidated his competition that in the 1980 Woodward Stakes no trainer would run a horse against him, and he ran by himself in an unusual one-horse race, a walkover.

Junior Racetrackers

Most jockeys have been exposed to horses from an early age, growing up on farms or near racetracks. Top jockey Angel Cordero, Jr., winner of three Kentucky Derbys, was the son of a jockey and trainer, Angel Cordero, Sr. The Corderos lived in a house near the track in Puerto Rico, and as a youngster Angel, Jr., enjoyed visiting the horses in the mornings with his uncle, Deo Cordero. When Angel, Jr., was six, his father bought him a pony so he could ride regularly. A great mimic, young Cordero observed stable routine and began treating the pony like a racehorse, bandaging his legs and giving him vitamins.

Earl Sande

John Longden

At age eight, Cordero helped his father by grooming some of the lesser horses in the barn, and at ten he was an exercise rider, principally with fillies. Three years later, when stronger physically, he was entrusted with exercising the colts. At fifteen, Cordero was getting on fifteen horses a morning, grooming several others between rides, and ponying horses to the track in the afternoons. After attending a school for jockeys, Cordero rode his first race at the age of eighteen. Many jockeys start even younger—Isaac Murphy began riding in races at fourteen and Eddie Arcaro at fifteen.

Bill Shoemaker was a ninety-pound member of his high school boxing team in California when he first became conscious of daily race results on the radio and of stories in the local paper about the exploits of the great Johnny Longden, the West's leading rider. Longden's popularity prompted many friends to comment that the four-foot-eleven-inch Shoemaker had the build of a jockey.

During Shoemaker's early rise to prominence, many trainers were hesitant to ride him despite his obvious talent, because his light weight required him to add so much lead. (Shoemaker was so small at birth—2½ pounds—that his grandmother put him in a shoebox and employed the family stove as an incubator.)

Veteran trainer Hurst Philpot, who hired Shoe as an exercise boy and hot-walker when he was seventeen, thought Shoemaker was too small to ever become a top rider and was reluctant to give him a chance. One of the first trainers who preferred Shoe with dead weight to some other jockeys with their live weight was Hall of Fame horseman Preston Burch. When Burch began putting Shoemaker on his good horses, others took note and began using him, too.

Shoemaker rode 219 winners in his first season in 1949 and quickly became known as a youngster who made horses run for him. In his second season he tied with Joe Culmone of New Jersey as America's leading jockey at 388 winners each. Their dramatic duel went down to the final day of the year.

The Great Athlete

What is it that makes a winning jockey? Athletic ability is certainly a plus, as demonstrated by the all-around athlete Bill Shoemaker, who has been called "pound for pound . . . the greatest jockey in the world" by the British racing journalist John Oaksey, watching Shoe competing in England in the Chivas Regal Challenge series. Dr. Robert Kerlan, the prominent orthopedic surgeon and a keen racing fan, says Shoemaker is one of the greatest athletes he has ever known. This is no idle compliment, for Dr. Kerlan has served as a consulting surgeon for Los Angeles professional teams—the Dodgers, the Rams, and the Lakers. Kerlan put Shoemaker through a series of tests organized by the National Athletic Health Institute and graded him—while Shoe was still in his forties—among the top 10 percent of mature athletes in muscle strength, endurance, and power. Dr. Kerlan said Shoe tested twenty years younger than his age.

An outstanding jockey invariably has excellent balance. The art of breaking a horse out of a gate alertly is a demanding test of balance, and balance is a key factor in helping a horse to settle in stride. Balance is critical, too, when setting a horse down for the drive. The top rider acts with his horse and not as a distracting force, helping him in every way possible.

Most top jockeys have a special rapport with horses—a "feel" for a horse. Shoemaker, for example, has developed great sensitivity with his hands. He has always been very light with the reins on a horse's sensitive mouth and blends himself skillfully with the horse's movements. Horses love to run for him, say the experts on the backstretch. Jockeys with this type of sensitivity can somehow understand what they have to do to get the very best out of an animal. These jockeys are worth their weight in gold.

The Right Horses

A jockey can be a wonderful rider, but without good horses he does not have a chance. To get talented

Eddie Arcaro

Jockey Silks

Tom Gentry
W.H. McCauley

Royal Lines,
Lessee
Sandy Hawley

Klein, French,
and Beal
Angel Cordero, Jr.

Edward Anchel
Richard Migliore

Eugene V. Klein
Gary Stevens

B. Levy and
Cisley Stable
Craig Perret

Peter M. Brant
Bill Shoemaker

H. DeKwiatkowski
Jerry D. Bailey

Peter M. Brant
Jacinto Vasquez

A.I. Appleton
Walter Guerra

Philip Teinowitz
José Santos

Ervin J. Kowitz
G.W. Hutton

D. and P.
Scharbauer
Chris McCarron

Chillingworth,
Duckett,
Winchell, et al.
Don Brumfield

Belles, Lessee,
and Leveton
Laffit Pincay, Jr.

T. B. Badgett
Mickey Solomone

Loblolly Stable
Pat Day

*Listed next to each jacket are the
names of the owner and the jockey in
the 113th Derby.*

horses, most jockeys have agents, who receive as much as 25 percent of the jockey's earnings. Since the jockey's earnings are based on the winning purses of the horses he rides, an agent benefits by lining up winners for his client. A good agent is familiar with the trainers and horses at a track and can choose appropriate horses for the jockey. He can also steer him away from dangerous horses and those whose forms are declining.

The right agent can make a tremendous difference in a jockey's career. Angel Cordero, Jr., landed the services of a top agent in 1967—Vince DeGregory, who helped him get rides on mounts that won him 277 races that year. The following year Cordero was the national champion, with 345 victories and purses in excess of $2.6 million.

Bill Shoemaker's career took off after he was introduced to a smart agent from New York, Harry Silbert. Silbert and Shoemaker discussed terms, shook hands, and maintained their relationship through Shoe's 8,700 winning rides until Silbert died of cancer at seventy-five in January 1987.

On Derby Day the nation's best jockeys are always in demand, and many of them like to hold off choosing their mounts until the last possible moment.

In 1959 Bill Shoemaker was trying to hold off from making a Derby commitment. A colt he had been riding, Tomy Lee, had been a top 2-year-old, but appeared not to have regained his form at 3. Frank Childs, Tomy Lee's trainer, approached Shoemaker's agent, Harry Silbert, with an offer: If Tomy Lee won his two races prior to the Derby, Shoe would ride him in the Run for the Roses. Silbert agreed after discussing it with Shoemaker.

Tomy Lee won both races, but not brilliantly. On the Saturday before the 85th Kentucky Derby, Shoemaker rode the fine colt Sword Dancer in the seven-furlong Stepping Stone Purse at Churchill Downs, replacing Sam Boulmetis, the colt's regular jockey. Sword Dancer led all the way and won smartly.

"See if you can get me off Tomy Lee," Shoemaker told Silbert that night. "I would prefer to ride Sword Dancer in the Derby."

"I can't do it, Bill," Silbert said. "I've spoken to Frank Childs and he insists we honor our commitment."

Thus it was that Shoemaker rode Tomy Lee in the Kentucky Derby of 1959, beating Bill Boland on Sword Dancer by a nose.

Purse-String Politics

Just as compatible agents and jockeys are crucial, so are trainer-and-jockey combinations: Ben and Jimmy Jones and Eddie Arcaro, Woody Stephens and Eddie Maple, Charlie Whittingham and Bill Shoemaker. Although in the past it was common for a jockey to be contracted to a particular stable— Eddie Arcaro, for example, was signed as a contract rider for Greentree Stable—most of today's jockeys are free agents, letting their agents select their mounts carefully and trying hard not to commit entirely to one stable or trainer. Some journeymen still ride for a particular trainer, and apprentice jockeys frequently do.

Naturally, competition for the top jockeys is spirited, and these jockeys are occasionally offered more than the regular percentage of the winnings to ride a particular horse. The usual arrangement today is that a jockey gets 10 percent of the purse his horse earns in stakes and 10 percent of first-place winnings in other races. When a jockey is contracted to ride in a stakes race, as a rule, his expenses, including travel, are paid. A jockey who wins a very big race may also see a tip, or bonus, in addition to his percentage.

Sharing the Wealth

When more than one horse represents a stable in a race, some trainers permit the riders to divide the 10-percent commission to the winning horse the way they want. In the Santa Anita Handicap of 1962, trainer Mesh Tenney saddled two horses for Rex Ellsworth, Prove It and Olden Times. Lin Boice,

who also trained for Ellsworth, had a horse of his own named Physician in the race. Because of the close association, the stewards insisted that the three horses race as a single entry.

Prove It, carrying under 126 pounds, was considered the main threat and was ridden by Bill Shoemaker. Olden Times, the speed of the race, was ridden by Alex Maese. Shoemaker's good friend Don Pierce got the mount on the mildly regarded Physician. When Shoe and Maese chatted that afternoon, they decided to split 50–50 if either of them won, leaving Pierce in the cold. Olden Times set the pace as expected and ran well. Prove It raced forwardly for the first mile but began to tire at the head of the stretch. Physician was last of thirteen starters for the first six furlongs, but then began to pick up momentum and pass horses with abandon.

In the upper stretch, as Prove It was stopping badly and Olden Times was running out of gas, Physician, in full stride, passed them both. As Pierce drove by, Shoe hollered, "We're cutting you back in!"

Pierce smiled, rode Physician to a 2½-length victory, and walked away from the postrace ceremonies figuring out what he would do with the entire 10 percent of the winner's share of $100,000.

Horse Sense

Not only must a jockey be allied with the right agent and trainer, he must also be intelligent. Eddie Arcaro, considered the greatest jockey America ever produced, was one of the smartest as well. Fans found his daring moves remarkable, but he never went for a hole between horses without an alternative, a contingency plan. Young riders, anxious to save ground, stop many a horse when a hole suddenly closes in front of them. And when stopped, the majority of horses cannot get going again in time to win. So an intelligent rider like Bill Shoemaker learns to lose ground and win races by taking the overland route—while also being ready to make a split-second decision to head through an opening when possible, as was the case in his

Bill Hartack on Majestic Prince in 1969

brilliant Derby ride on Ferdinand in 1986.

Isaac Murphy's great versatility won him many a race. A jockey who wasn't afraid to change tactics when appropriate, he was known for his patience and ability to wait as long as possible before asking his horses to run. However, midrace in the American Derby of 1886, Murphy suddenly spurred his horse, Silver Cloud, into high gear, sent him to a substantial lead, and then nursed his margin the rest of the way to win. Ben Ali, the Kentucky Derby winner of that year, was among the many outstanding runners to be upset that day by Murphy's seizing the initiative.

Five-time Derby winner Bill Hartack made a point of preparing for his work very diligently. He studied the "past performances" in *Daily Racing Form* thoroughly to note speed and peculiarities and paid close attention to his fellow riders, noting their habits and their styles. He knew when they were likely to move on a horse and what they would usually do in most circumstances.

The Will to Win

In the end, though, it is a jockey's drive—his will to win—that distinguishes him among his peers. Bill Hartack rode five Kentucky Derby winners in his first nine attempts, and in none of these victories was he on a horse who was pound-for-pound the best in the field. He asked the best not only of himself, but also of his mounts. Or rather, he insisted on the best and would not settle for less. He had no great affection for the horses he rode. He was simply on a mission. They were part of the team. They would carry out their assignments. He thought he should win with every horse he ever rode.

Once, when Hartack was riding for Calumet Farm, Jimmy Jones put him on a horse who had been away from racing for a long period because of injury. Jones told Hartack to get what he could, but not to punish the horse severely. Hartack was furious. "If you don't want me to win, don't put me on him," he told an astonished Jones in the paddock. "I only

know one way to ride and that's to get everything I can out of every horse."

Cordero's Drive

As the third-winningest jockey in racing history, Angel Cordero, Jr., is also well known for his drive to be victorious. On occasion his zeal has made him a national villain. The most celebrated incident occurred in 1980, when he rode Codex to victory in the Preakness Stakes.

Codex appeared to be best that day and the consensus is that he would probably have won under any circumstances. But Cordero, riding on the lead entering the stretch, turned in the saddle and looked back to locate the principal threat, the filly Genuine Risk, who had won the Kentucky Derby. Cordero permitted Codex to drift out, carrying Genuine Risk extremely wide and causing her to break stride. Codex went on to win by almost five lengths.

As soon as he passed the winning post, outraged fans from across the country who saw the race on television inundated the Pimlico switchboard with furious criticism of Cordero's tactics. A stewards' hearing was followed by a lengthy hearing conducted by the Maryland Racing Commission, but no action was taken against Codex or Cordero. There were more cries of outrage leveled at Cordero in 1983 after Caveat's victory in the Belmont Stakes that year. Caveat, second choice in the race, was trained by Woody Stephens and ridden by Laffit Pincay, Jr. Coming from off the pace, he was moving to the leaders in the upper stretch when Pincay decided to send him along the rail through a narrow opening inside Au Point and the favorite, Slew o'Gold, ridden by Cordero.

It was a risky maneuver because of the size of the hole, and Pincay might have been wiser to go to the outside. Caveat moved toward the opening, and Cordero, riding Slew o'Gold just outside of Au Point, moved to shut the hole. He began squeezing Gregg McCarron inside of him on Au Point. Caveat, who had just moved abreast of the two leaders, was

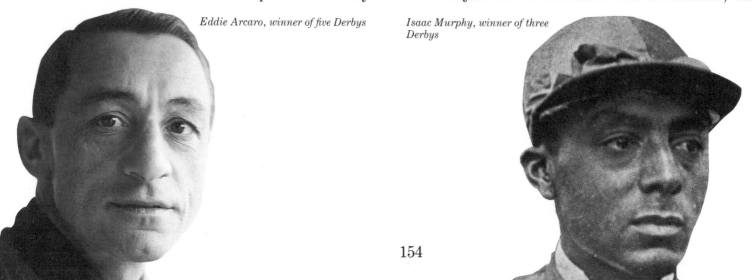

Eddie Arcaro, winner of five Derbys

Isaac Murphy, winner of three Derbys

154

pushed into the fence. He recovered quickly and went on to win by 3½ lengths. Subsequent X rays, however, revealed that the horse had damaged an ankle in the contretemps, and he never raced again. Furious, Stephens vowed never to ride Cordero again—and he has kept his pledge.

Risky Business

Cordero's daring places him at risk. In 1986 he missed the Derby because he was in physical therapy, recovering from a bad fall in which he was seriously injured. Cordero rebounded remarkably in the summer to capture his eleventh riding title at the prestigious Saratoga meeting.

Rough riding is risky riding. Jockeys know there is always the chance that their horse may fall, even when they are riding perfectly. When 1,000 pounds of horse is traveling at full speed, a fall can be deadly. A good jockey can usually sense when his mount is hurt and is skilled at pulling a horse up safely. However, there is often no warning before a horse goes down, and very few riders have not suffered some sort of injury at the track. To avoid injury a jockey must be able to react quickly—and correctly. A moment's hesitation and the horse and rider can fall.

In 1987 when Alysheba almost fell after entering the stretch on his winning drive in the Kentucky Derby, his quick-thinking jockey, Chris McCarron, did far more than rescue the colt to win America's premier race: He averted a catastrophe. Had Alysheba fallen, a number of the horses and jockeys would have gone down, and it is likely some would not have made it back up.

Triple Crown Fracture

Bill Hartack lost the mount on Kentucky Derby and Preakness winner Tim Tam in the 1958 Classics because of a freak accident. On the Saturday before the Derby—opening day at the Downs—Hartack rode a 2-year-old filly, Quail Egg, for his good friend Henry Forrest. Riding 2-year-olds in the spring is a hazardous business, for they are very green and

excitable. The filly went into the air in the starting gate and mashed Hartack's leg against the side of the gate. It required no X rays for the rider to realize that the leg was fractured, and he was rushed to the hospital. Several days later he was released, a cast on his broken leg. He watched from the press box as Tim Tam, under Milo Valenzuela, won the 84th Run for the Roses.

Hartack watched on television two weeks later as Tim Tam captured the Preakness under Valenzuela, beating Lincoln Road, the same horse he had beaten in the Derby.

Nine days later, Hartack appeared at Garden State Park, where the main division of Calumet Farm was stabled. Doctors had removed the heavy cast from his leg and outfitted him with a light brace encased in leather so he would have mobility. He told trainer Jimmy Jones he was ready to ride, accepted a few mounts, and the following week rode Iron Liege to finish fourth in the Camden Handicap.

The Belmont Stakes was to be run the following week, and Hartack was anxious to ride Tim Tam in the race. Jones was in a bind. He felt an obligation to Valenzuela, who had ridden the colt to win the Derby and Preakness. He told Hartack that if Tim Tam won, he would receive 10 percent of the purse, the same honorarium Valenzuela would receive. Hartack said he would not accept the money if he could not ride the horse.

Jones was uncertain of his course of action, when a cable arrived from Calumet's owner, Mrs. Gene Markey, in Paris. She said she hoped Jones would use Valenzuela in the Belmont, and that settled the matter. That Saturday Tim Tam was moving to the leader when he fractured a sesamoid at the head of the stretch. Gamely, he finished second, but the dream of a Triple Crown was gone.

To make the occasion less painful and to cheer him up, Mrs. Markey sent Hartack a check for $5,000. He never acknowledged the gift, nor did he cash it, causing considerable furor with Mrs. Markey's books and her bank. He announced the following week that his association with Calumet Farm was

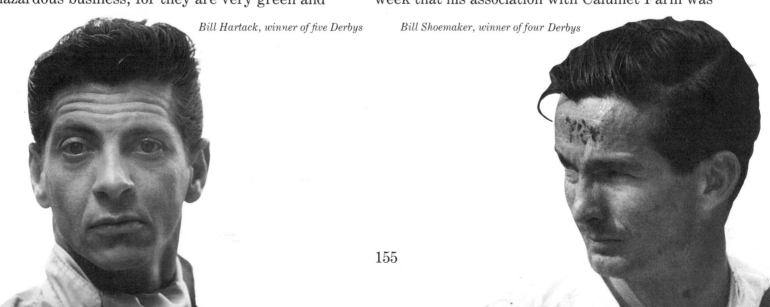

Bill Hartack, winner of five Derbys   *Bill Shoemaker, winner of four Derbys*

over, and he rode as a free-lancer throughout the remainder of his career.

A Dangerous Profession

Bill Shoemaker suffered his first major injury in 1968, when he fractured his right thighbone in a spill at Santa Anita. A stainless steel rod was inserted down the middle of the leg to stabilize the fracture, and Shoe was out of action for thirteen months. The day he came back he rode three winners, two of them saddled by Charlie Whittingham, and the crowd at Santa Anita was moved to applause and tears on an afternoon of unrivaled emotion.

It was only months later that a young horse flipped over backward in the paddock at Hollywood Park, shattering Shoemaker's pelvis and badly bruising his bladder. At thirty-eight, he had every reason to take honorable leave of a dangerous profession. But he was determined to come back, and four months later he was riding again, in better form than ever.

For Ron Turcotte, rider of the 1973 Triple Crown winner, Secretariat, and 1972 Derby winner, Riva Ridge, there was to be no rebound from a fall on July 13, 1978, at Belmont Park. When a horse named Flag of Leyte Gulf fell and threw him, breaking his back, Turcotte was left paralyzed and confined to a wheelchair. His life since then has been one of constant pain. What keeps him going is the memory of the 1973 Derby—and Secretariat.

"I dream of him sometimes. Not long ago . . . I dreamed that he had come back to racing and that I could walk and that I rode him again. It was a tremendous sensation. In a dream like that, you hear and see everything. He had a big neck, a long neck, and I remember riding him and looking between his ears. It was like the Kentucky Derby. I came from behind, and I won."

They are little men. Bill Shoemaker weighed 2½ pounds at birth and the doctor said he wouldn't live through the night. The baby's grandmother didn't agree. She put the tiny infant in a shoebox and kept him warm in a kitchen oven. When Shoemaker won the 1986 Derby at age fifty-four, he had grown to four-foot-eleven and ninety-six pounds.

Jockeys are little men dressed in colored silks. They sit atop a horse so lightly as to seem made of air. These are men not much more than five feet tall. They may weigh 112 pounds, but they'd rather be lighter.

The horse is a half-ton animal flying up to forty miles an hour. At the rail during a race, you feel thunder drumming up from the earth. It is a mismatch, the little man and the big horse. Against a horse's strength, a jockey has no answer. He must use other tools.

Shoemaker's "touch" is the envy of all jockeys. The little man, as if by magic, can persuade a horse to run where it doesn't want to run and run there faster than it ever has before. To see Laffit Pincay, Jr., without a shirt on is to know that strength is part of the jock's package, for Pincay is a miniature Mr. Universe. Touch and strength. With not just a clock in his head, but a computer, too. Only the brightest jockeys find a way through the permutations of a race.

The permutations have one constant. Danger. These little men are unique in all of sport. They are afloat on air but full of thunder. We read about "spills," and the word sounds so soft. "Spills," as if the jockey has been a teacup of milk spilled onto a lace napkin. No. We're talking about half-ton animals in a cavalry charge. A man is slammed to the earth and caught under a stampede's hooves.

These are not little men. These are big little men.

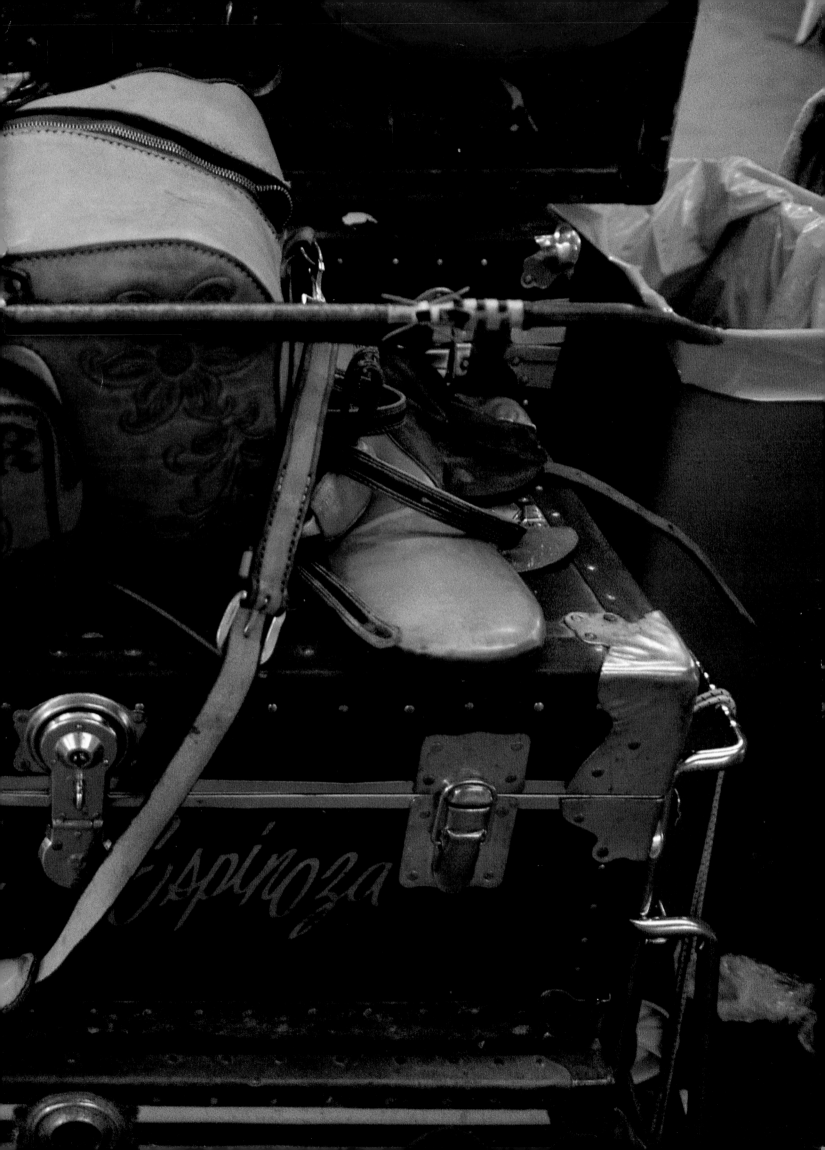

Boots shining. Helmet ready. A jockey may work bush tracks and bullrings, little circles of hellish risk where he might make twenty-five dollars a day. First time he wins a race, the old hands turn him upside down in a barrel and beat its sides with baseball bats. Now, at last, he's on a Derby horse.

A jock's life is hard for a hundred reasons—from weight to fear to loneliness. He first must be a good athlete—with strength and balance, flexibility and endurance. For the best, there is fame. Others live on the edge.

Charlie Mueller moonlighted as a plumber. He rode in the '83 Derby and came in fifteenth. "All those years watching it on TV, I wondered what it'd be like to be here. . . . I loved it."

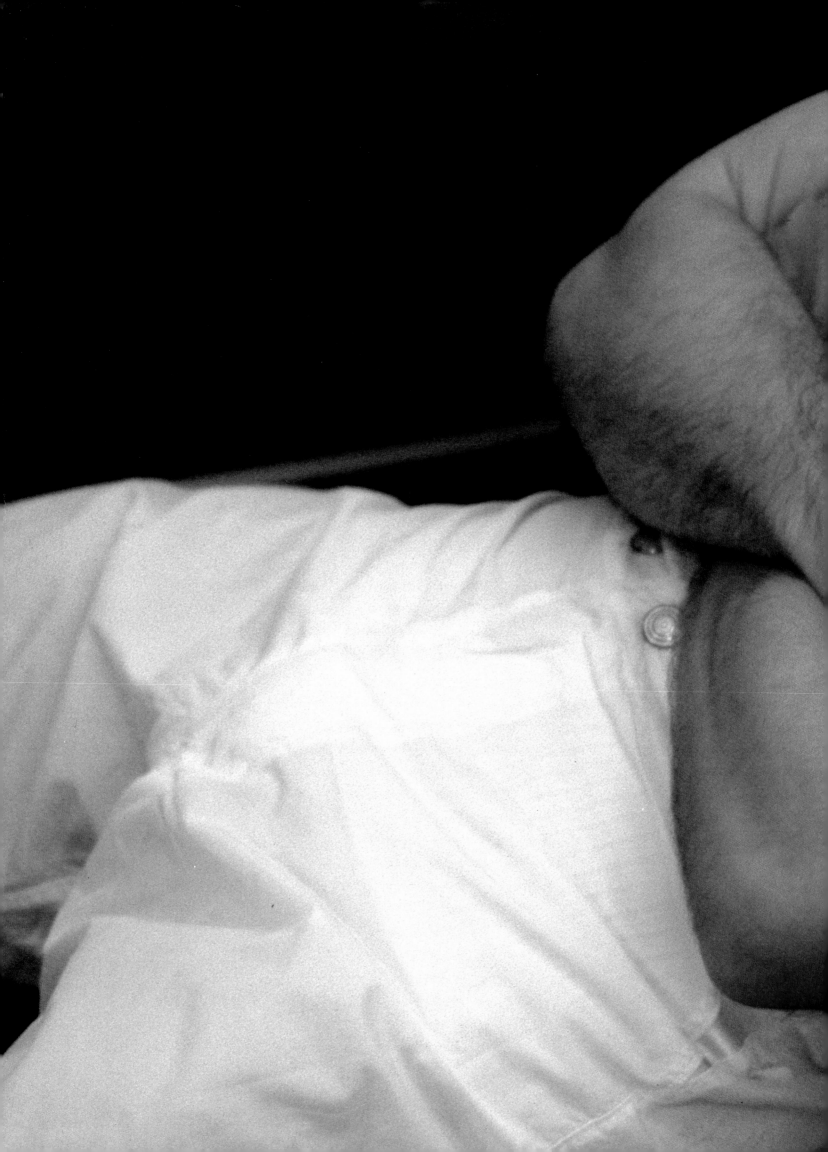

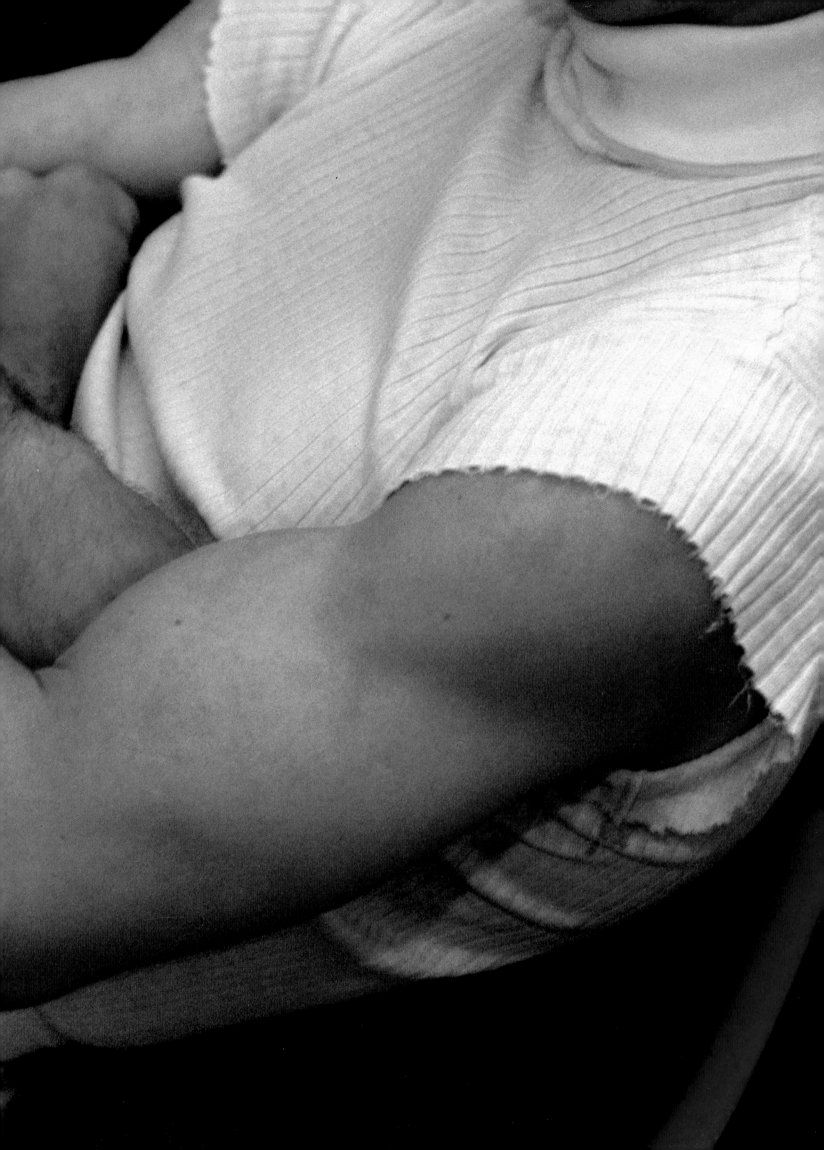

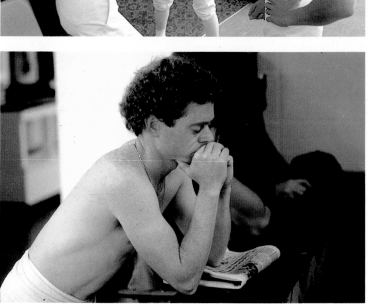

The jocks' room. It's home when a jock can't be home. Between races, the riders rest here. They dress here. They play pool, ping-pong, cards, craps. They watch TV. They study. They think.

Here, Sam Maple (top) and Daryl Montoya (above) relax.

In their room, jocks like Pat Day (top right) rehash races or, like Chris McCarron (above right), commune in silence.

They're gypsies, most of them, moving from track to track, following the work. Only the richest and most famous can pick their jobs. Lesser jocks scuffle for rides.

They're Latins and poor boys out of ranch lands. They're kids who want to escape the Kentucky coal mines. They grew up small and everyone said, "You a jockey?"

A small boy named Laffit Pincay, Jr., (page 174) asked to be put on a horse, and of that moment when he first sat up there, Pincay would say, "The horse, he so high."

They do it at first because it is something they can do. They were given the body for it. Steve Cauthen may have been given more than that. His father was a rider and later a farrier; his mother was a trainer. As if by inheritance, the boy came to the track supernaturally calm. At sixteen he was a star, New York's leading rider. At eighteen he won the Triple Crown on Affirmed.

They know the danger. Jorge Velasquez (top) has been under the horses. Bill Shoemaker (above) spent six months in a body cast after a horse reared in the paddock and fell on him, crushing his pelvis. He rode within a year.

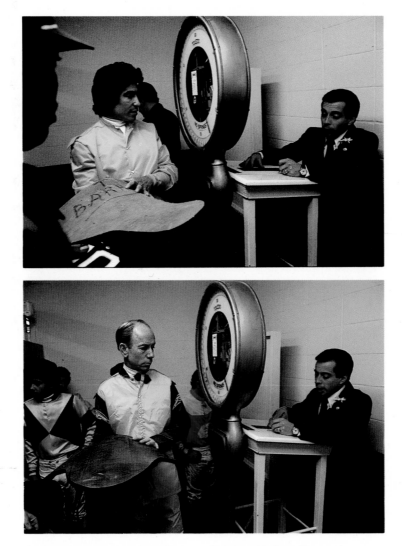

Weighing out for the Derby. Before leaving for the paddock, jockeys weigh with their tack for the clerk of scales. The Derby weight of 126 pounds doesn't include the helmet, about a pound. Five-foot-two Chris McCarron (opposite) weighed 109 pounds for his victorious ride on Alysheba in 1987.

In 1971 Robert Parrott became the second overweight rider in Derby history. He put 127 pounds on Saigon Warrior, who finished twentieth and last.

Laffit Pincay, Jr. (left top), on a plane flight coast to coast, once requested a peanut as dinner. He spread a napkin, picked up a knife, and sliced the peanut into quarters. He made the meal last an hour.

After winning the '66 Derby, Don Brumfield (left bottom) proclaimed himself "the happiest hillbilly hardboot you'll ever see." He later said he celebrated that night by splurging at dinner. He put dressing on his salad.

Of all riders, it seems, only Shoemaker has never been in the steam room losing weight to work. They call it "the hot box." It has driven many jocks out of the business. It has done worse, too. A steady occupant, Howard Grant, said, "The box'll fry your brain."

Raised in Louisiana's bayou country, Eddie Delahoussaye (overleaf) must also watch his weight and curb his keen appetite for Cajun dishes.

Mint Juleps & Other Southern Comforts

When the gates of Churchill Downs first opened on May 17, 1875, the day of the inaugural Kentucky Derby, the eyes of the racing community throughout the country were focused on twenty-nine-year-old Meriwether Lewis Clark, Jr., and his ambitious project to establish a classic American race in the tradition of England's Epsom Derby. At the day's end, Aristides had become the first horse to win the Kentucky Derby, and Clark had secured a niche in racing history.

Clark's Luck

Three years earlier a group of breeders, some on the verge of abandoning their operations, convinced Clark, a Louisville socialite and the grandson of William Clark of the famous Lewis and Clark expedition, to help resurrect racing in Louisville. Since he had no background in the management of a racetrack, Clark set out for Europe on a scouting mission of his own to study racing.

After nearly two years of research abroad, Clark returned to Louisville and summoned the breeders to a meeting. There he outlined his plan for the establishment of a racetrack in Louisville and the formation of a permanent series of races modeled after the English classics; he also envisioned the creation of the greatest race of all, patterned after the Epsom Derby, to be called the Kentucky Derby.

Clark's enthusiasm was boundless. In 1874 he formed a corporation formally known as the Louisville Jockey Club and Driving Park Association, raised $32,000, and selected a track site just a few miles south of the heart of the city. The property selected was owned by Clark's two uncles, John and Henry Churchill, who permitted Clark to lease the land rather than purchase it outright. However, after the land was cleared and the one-mile racing strip was graded and constructed, the funds were exhausted. And still there was no grandstand. W.H. Thomas, a prominent Louisville merchant, came to the rescue, loaning the track enough money to build a small wooden grandstand.

Although just a young man, Clark handled the first Derby Day like a pro. In the following two decades of his tenure as track president, Clark became the best-known man in Louisville, and his Derby its best-loved race. In fact, everything at Churchill Downs seemed to center around Clark. On Derby Day patrons were fond of predicting "Clark Weather," meaning fair, sunny skies. "Clark Luck" was said to account for such weather. And the day of the Clark Stakes was known as "Clark Day."

Horse Sense

Clark, who became known as a "colonel" in the finest Kentucky tradition, used good, old-fashioned common sense in running the racetrack. For example, he did all he could to attract ladies to the track, reasoning that if they enjoyed themselves at the races, they would encourage their husbands' patronage. He also was not afraid to voice his opinion, even if it was not a popular one. To wit, he believed turf writers should refrain from betting, as he felt it would influence their objectivity in reporting.

Yet Clark was extremely popular with the writers. He would invite the newsmen to the clubhouse for a drink, and he would praise them for accurate reporting. On Derby Day the newspapers documented his every move.

A man with a taste for sparkling champagne, Clark liked to throw parties and dinners. He was a big spender—and a big man, weighing as much as 300 pounds. His dinners were the talk of the town.

An Era Ends

For all the fun Clark had running the Derby, the track was a financial failure. Clark did what he could to keep it going, including spending his own money to cover losses. Sadly, after a financially disastrous 1894 spring meeting, the Clark regime ended, and Churchill Downs was sold to a group headed by William Schulte, a Louisville racehorse owner and bookmaker, who immediately constructed a new 1,500-seat grandstand on the opposite side of the track from where the original stands had been; in the old structure, patrons had faced the sun. Atop the new grandstand Schulte erected two tall spires, distinctive structures that are still the track's trademark. As for Colonel Clark, he was retained as presiding judge, a position he held until 1899, when he committed suicide.

Playing a Longshot

In the 1890s and the early years of this century, the future of the Derby was in jeopardy. Churchill Downs continued to lose money, and the outlook became so bleak following the 1902 Derby that it seemed likely the track would be permanently closed.

Enter Colonel Matt Winn. A chubby, pink-faced cigar-smoker best described as looking "something like Alfred Hitchcock, with a bit of W.C. Fields thrown in," Winn was a Louisville tailor and, like Clark, had no previous experience in racetrack management. Nevertheless, he had the imagination and determination to resuscitate the ailing track. The preservation of the Derby was of extreme importance to him, because Winn had always been a Derby fan. As a boy, he had watched the inaugural running in 1875 from the seat of his father's flatbed grocery wagon in the infield—and he never missed a Derby thereafter for the rest of his life. Winn also enjoyed betting, particularly on long shots. Saving the Derby was a long shot he could not resist. With the Derby's future in his hands, Winn helped form a syndicate of Louisvillians to put up $40,000 to purchase the track. Charles F. Grainger, mayor

of Louisville, was named track president and Winn vice president. Then in late 1903 Grainger and the others asked Winn to take over as general manager.

The Great Beginner

Although Winn initially expressed reluctance to launch a new career at the age of forty-two, his lack of background in racetrack management did not scare him, because, as he put it, "I didn't know anything about clothing when I became a tailor. I'm a great beginner." More than that, he was a great promoter. And it turned out he was the perfect man for the job.

If ever there was a man ahead of his time in the field of promotion, it was Matt Winn. He had the mind of a businessman and the flair of a publicity man. When Winn's group took over, the Derby was not receiving the local support it once had from prominent Louisvillians. To change this, the new management decided to build a $20,000 frame clubhouse, which they financed by offering memberships to 200 high-ranking Louisvillians at a cost of $100 each.

A personable individual whom a friend once decribed as the only Irish diplomat in existence, Winn could also be a fighter. Whenever a business battle erupted, he was not afraid to step in and go to war. One of the most important battles Winn fought in those early years came in 1908, when a new city administration, hostile to Winn's aims, arranged to pass a law prohibiting bookmaking. Since pari-mutuel betting was legal, he proceeded to round up eleven old pari-mutuel machines for the 1908 meeting, running it on schedule. Following this Derby, pari-mutuel wagering, which had been all but ignored in America for more than thirty years, was eventually accepted throughout the country.

A Higher-Quality Field

It took several years for Winn to get the Derby rolling into high gear. Although the race had attracted eastern attention in its first dozen years, when Winn's group took over the Derby had become

Winners of the first Derby in 1875

primarily a provincial event. That changed in 1911, when easterner R.F. Carman, frustrated by a two-year shutdown of New York racing, sent his fine colt Meridian to Louisville and won the Derby. The triumphant Meridian went on to earn acclaim as the best 3-year-old of 1911. In 1912 a New Yorker also won the renewal.

The next year the fact that the winner, Donerail, came rolling home at a whopping $184.90 straight payoff did not hurt the race from a headline standpoint, nor did the fact that he set a track record in doing so. The following year Old Rosebud, the 2-year-old champion of 1913, roared to a blazing victory in 2:03⅖, shattering Donerail's record of the year before. Winn made good use of these two races to promote the Derby in 1915 as "America's greatest race."

The Derby's First Filly

Gaining more publicity for the race, Regret made Derby history in 1915 by becoming the first filly to win. Winn, in recalling the race years later, said that it "needed only a victory by Regret to create for us some coast-to-coast publicity, and Regret did not fail us. The Derby thus was made an American institution."

Page One Victory

But Winn did not rest on his laurels. He kept after the major stables to bring their top horses to the Derby and, in 1922, scored a promotional coup. Morvich, a horse mentioned at the time in the same breath with Man o' War, was the undefeated 2-year-old champion of 1921. That year the Derby and the Preakness were scheduled for the same day. The racing world was abuzz with the big question: Would Morvich go to Baltimore rather than Louisville? Two months before the Derby, Winn declared that Morvich would run for the roses. As promised, Morvich arrived at Louisville—and won the Derby. Out-of-town reporters converged in droves at Churchill Downs to write about the heralded colt.

The Diamond Jubilee Party

A fixture at Churchill Downs, Winn served as track president from 1938 to 1949—although he had been a power since his arrival at the Downs in the early 1900s. Known as "Mr. Derby," Winn looked forward with particular pleasure to seeing the 1949 Diamond Jubilee Derby.

Despite a serious illness in 1947, Winn lived to see the 1949 renewal, won by the famed Calumet Farm's Ponder. But the Diamond Jubilee Derby was to be the Colonel's last. He passed away on October 6, 1949, at the age of eighty-eight.

New Faces

Succeeding Winn was the raspy-voiced Bill Corum, a popular syndicated New York columnist and well-known radio sports announcer who loved racing best. As Downs president, he continued writing his column in New York, but each spring he took a leave of absence to perform his duties at the Derby.

In 1959 Wathen Knebelkamp became Downs president, and nobody had ever been better prepared for the job than he. A distinguished and astute Louisville businessman, Knebelkamp had an extensive background in racing. Under his supervision Churchill Downs underwent a long-overdue renovation. Some $9 million was spent to build the fourth-floor Skye Terrace, a plush box-seat area; new jockeys' quarters; new pressbox; a glass-enclosed box section on the fifth floor; a sprinkler system for the entire grandstand; and several new restaurants and bars. He redid the stable area, converting many of the tack rooms from wood to concrete block, and he also expanded the Churchill Downs staff.

Knebelkamp's favorite Derby was the 1969 running, which President Richard Nixon attended. It had been Knebelkamp's goal to have a president attend the Derby, to "help the image of horse racing." When Knebelkamp retired that December 31, he had gone over nine years without a vacation.

Meriwether Lewis Clark

Colonel Matt Winn

A Tradition Grows

The next president, forty-four-year-old Lynn Stone, was a New Orleans native who had grown up in California. He had come to Louisville in the late fifties as a minor league baseball executive and a bank administrator, and went to work at Churchill Downs in 1961. Five years later he was named vice president and general manager.

During Stone's regime, improvements continued at Churchill Downs. Steel emergency stairways were constructed in the back of the stands, and an ambitious renovation of the stable area was completed. The Derby continued to grow, too, drawing a record crowd of 163,628 for the centennial running in 1974. The Downs also added more racing days to its calendar.

After fifteen years Stone resigned as Downs president, when stock dividends were diluted by disastrous summer racing, and was succeeded by Tom Meeker. A lawyer practicing in Louisville, Meeker was named permanent president at the age of forty-one, the track's youngest leader since Clark.

A Bright Future

Originally from Oklahoma, Meeker was named general counsel for the Downs in 1981. When the track was threatened by two takeover attempts in 1984, Meeker helped organize its successful defense strategy.

Once Meeker became Downs president, he started working to improve the track's community image, and he launched a five-year, $25-million renovation program that included a new turf course, open in the spring of 1987, as well as a $2.6 million paddock and tote board complex. At the dedication ceremony for the new paddock area, he said, "We bid farewell to that old and historic paddock where so many great horses had been saddled for the Kentucky Derby. Today begins a new era . . . ." Meeker, with an eye to the future, was paying tribute to the golden legacy of Meriwether Lewis Clark.

The swirling kaleidoscope dazzles and beguiles, a thousand colors changing places and forms in the seducing sunlight of May's first Saturday. And with every rearrangement of color comes a new mix of sound. We hear drums. A trombone. There is the hum of the multitude gathered, a river of sound flowing gently, softly. We're moving downstream on this river of sound. We hear a roar from somewhere, distant now but distinct. And it never stops. It only comes nearer. Until we are inside the roar. And inside the colors.

At the Super Bowl, you never see the rising sun or feel damp clay tugging at your boots. The Kentucky Derby brings you into the rhythms of life, up against the very smells of earth.

Somehow, you spend a week in Louisville for the Derby and you leave feeling right good about humankind. Detroit burned when the Tigers won the World Series. Police with machine guns ringed a soccer field when Italy won the World Cup.

Irvin S. Cobb, the 1930s country philosopher, of Paducah, Kentucky, said he couldn't explain the magic of the Derby. "If I could do that, I'd have a larynx of spun silver and the tongue of an angel. But if you can, imagine a track that's like a bracelet of molten gold encircling a greensward that's like a patch of emerald velvet. . . ." And so on, about pretty women and brocaded terraces and speeding kings of the turf, until at last Cobb wrote, "But what's the use? Until you've been to Kentucky and with your own eyes beheld the Derby, you ain't never been nowheres and you ain't never seen nothin'!"

They come from everywhere. They sleep on the ground if they must. Customers at the World Series come with passionate attachments to the teams, just as the Super Bowl draws zealots of all persuasions. Not the Derby. Certainly some Derby folks know which horses are running. But it's not required reading. All that is required is a capacity for fun. Bring a tent. Bring the lawn chairs and a cooler. Some aspirin, too.

The gates are open for the sprint to the infield. Every year 70,000 people go into the middle of the Churchill Downs racecourse. From there you can see almost nothing. A flash of a horse as he passes, no more. But that's not the point. This is the Derby, the sun is shining, and if you have to be someplace, Churchill Downs is a good place to be.

*Old wooden grandstands
with brick walkways mark
Churchill Downs as a
charming anachronism in a
world of plastic and chrome.
From this uneven brick path
to the raucous infield, it's
only two flights up to the
ritzy box seats occupied by
people whose printed name
cards sometimes read "Polk
Laffoon III" or perhaps
"G. Breaux Ballard III." The
sixth floor is Millionaire's
Row, where everyone is
someone trying to be
unforgettable.*

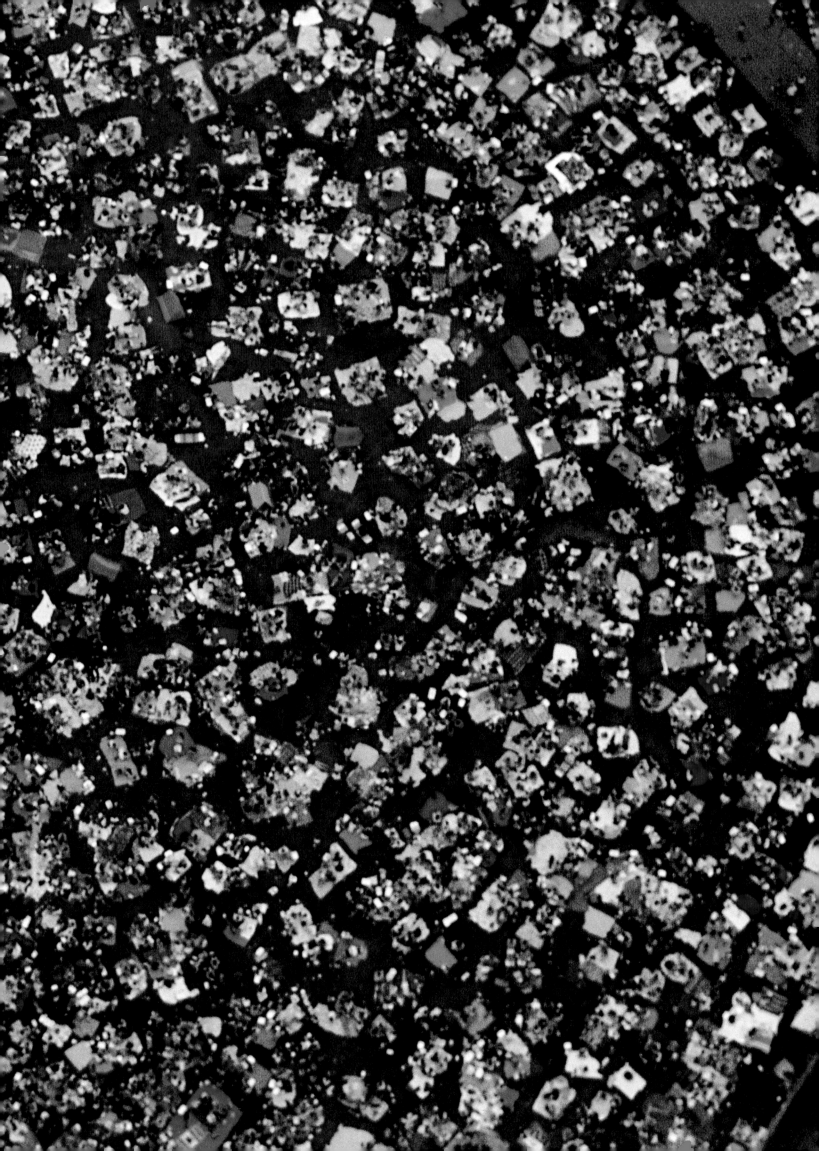

It's a violation of the law to bring liquor to the track on Derby Day. Perhaps it's so the track can make money selling you theirs. Those who do bring their own must resort to deceits, such as a hollow loaf of bread.

Ice cream, hot dogs, and mint juleps. Only at the Derby can a fun-lover suffer so. A mint julep is Kentucky bourbon sharing a glass with a sprig of mint and a ton of sugar.

The rich are different from you and me, Scott Fitzgerald told us. For a reminder we only have a step up to Millionaire's Row. No hollow loaves of bread here. All crystal and linen.

At the Derby everyone wears a hat. For ladies, flowers. For gents, straw. But alas, nary a Derby derby in sight.

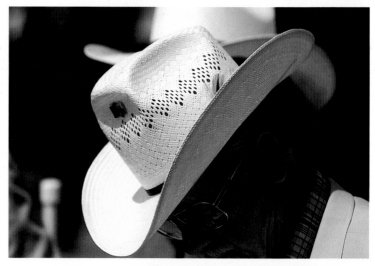

Win, Place, Show

n 1889 Frank James, whose younger brother, Jesse, made a name for himself in the railroad business, attended the Kentucky Derby prepared to do battle. With bookies, that is. Looking like a Southern gentleman in his Prince Albert suit and soft white hat, James won $2,400 on an early race on the card, then asked a bookmaker the price on Spokane in the Derby.

"Ten-to-one, and the sky's the limit," the bookie replied. James slapped down $5,000 on Spokane, and the bookie declared, "As far as I'm concerned, that's the sky."

James won his bet as Spokane nosed out the odds-on favorite, Proctor Knott, who bolted at the top of the stretch and raced down the straightaway on the extreme outside.

Bookmaking was legal in those days, which was more than could be said for the way the James boys sometimes made their living.

The Arrival of Pari-Mutuels

When the first Derby was run on May 17, 1875, two forms of wagering were in operation—the Paris Mutuals (later called pari-mutuels) from France and the auction pools. The latter accounted for most of the $50,000 wagered on the four races that were run that day. In the auction-pool system of wagering, an auctioneer would receive an opening bid, and then the auction would continue until the final bid was made on a horse. The person who made the last bid had that particular horse running for him. The track itself did not supervise the betting. Instead, it sold the wagering concessions to an outfit that came in and operated the betting.

In time the auction pools and Paris Mutuals disappeared, and bookmaking took over. In 1908 a new city administration passed a law making bookmaking illegal. For a while the law appeared to doom Churchill Downs because there was no other form of betting at the track. But after extensive research, Churchill Downs's ever-thinking Matt Winn uncovered a loophole in the law and established pari-mutuel wagering for the 1908 Derby. Management decided to sell $5.00 pari-mutuel tickets only, and this betting setup met with immediate approval from the 1908 crowd, particularly those who had Derby winner Stone Street at a $123.60 payoff.

In pari-mutuel wagering, the odds are made by the bettors themselves. The more money wagered on a particular horse, the lower the odds. The less bet on another horse, the higher the odds. The bettors are wagering against the judgment of others who are wagering, and the track, as stakeholder, receives a percentage of those bets.

For years the minimum bet at the Derby has been $2.00. In 1913 a $2.00 bet on long-shot winner Donerail resulted in a payoff of $184.90, a Derby record.

Lucky Long Shots

Another form of betting on the Derby is the winter book, or future book, conducted in Nevada and Mexico. In the winter book, a bettor wagers on a horse well in advance of the Derby, usually at odds higher than the horse will go off at on the first Saturday in May. The catch, however, is that if the horse does not go to the post in the Derby, the bettor does not get his money back. So every time a well-backed horse falls by the wayside on the road to the Derby, bookies win in a big way.

But the bookies can lose in a big way, too. For years, Black Gold's victory in the 1924 Derby was remembered as a dark day for bookmakers throughout the country. The public sent Black Gold off as the favorite on Derby Day, but this colt had been anything but a favorite in the winter book earlier in the year. The Derby's Big Three at that time was made up of Sarazen, unbeaten in ten starts as a 2-year-old and heavily backed for the race throughout the winter; Wise Counsellor, who was labeled the "pride of the Middle West"; and St.

James, owned by George D. Widener.
Black Gold started off in the winter book as a long shot, some bookies offering odds as high as 100–1 on the colt. As betting support started to show up on Black Gold, his odds gradually dropped from 50–1 to 20–1 to 10–1 and then 8–1. The bookies, though, were not particularly concerned about Black Gold, because the Big Three were still on the scene. However, all three dropped out of the Derby picture for various reasons, and when Black Gold ended up as the favorite on Derby Day, the bookies could not lay off any money, not at the high odds that they had laid on him. When Black Gold finished running that Derby Day, the bookies started running.

Big Payoffs

Many big bets have been cashed on the Derby, including the $150,000 reportedly won by Kansas City merchant prince Herbert Woolf when his Lawrin won the 1938 Kentucky Derby. He expressed his delight by giving trainer Ben Jones 20 percent of the purse, instead of the usual 10 percent. Colonel E.R. Bradley reputedly collected another big one in 1926 when his Bubbling Over won the race. Among his bets that day was an $85,000 horse-and-horse wager—Bubbling Over against W.R. Coe's Pompey, the best 2-year-old colt in the land the previous season.

With even more money on the line in other bets, Bradley gave his jockey, Albert Johnson, extra incentive by telling him that if Bubbling Over won the race, the rider would receive a large bonus. Bubbling Over won by five lengths, and Pompey came in fifth. The bottom line for Bradley? Well, this much is certain: He received $50,075 for Bubbling Over's win and $6,000 for stablemate Bagenbaggage's second-place finish, plus the $5,000 Derby cup. As for his various bets, it was said that Bradley won $250,000.

Past Performances

When it comes to wagering, most bettors rely on *Daily Racing Form*'s listing of past performances to tell them how a horse has been running. With each horse, the *Form* goes back a certain number of races (for the Derby, the entire career is shown) and lists such information as the date and track for each race; the distance; the track condition (muddy or fast, for example); certain fractions preceding the final time; the name of the race; the horse's post position; various calls during the running of the race designating a horse's position as the race progresses, including the margin by which he is either leading or trailing the leader; the horse's finish position; his jockey; the weight the horse carried; his odds; speed ratings (a number denoting how the horse's time compared with the track record); the one-two-three finishers; a comment by the chart-caller (such as "drew clear" or "bumped"); and the number of starters in the race. The *Form* also lists distances and times of recent workouts for the horses.

Serious bettors study the *Form* and take as many factors as possible—breeding, track condition, jockey—into consideration before putting their money down on a horse. Bettors are also alert for changes in equipment on a horse or for the type of medication when that information is available. Some states outlaw drugs that are legal in other jurisdictions. Bettors also like to watch a horse in the paddock or during the post parade.

Hot Tips

At Derby time, all a person has to do is listen to hear plenty of tips on the big race. The trick is to know whom to listen to. An individual whose opinion is particularly meaningful is Don DeWitt, one of the most knowledgeable and astute handicappers in the business. DeWitt's selections are among those appearing in the *Louisville Daily Sports News*, known around town for years as "the finger sheet." DeWitt's pick in each race is designated by the form of a finger pointing at the horse he selects. In 1986 the finger was alongside Ferdinand with the comment: "Strong as a bull in the final quarter mile." Which was exactly right.

Early purses on exhibit in the Kentucky Derby Museum

Exacta Wagering

Beginning with the 1985 renewal, exacta wagering has been held on the Derby, meaning that besides the traditional win, place, and show format, the bettors also have the chance to wager on the first two finishers in the race—in their exact order. In 1987 the exacta of Alysheba, an 8–1 shot, and Bet Twice, 10–1 in the betting, produced a payoff of $109.60.

A Pocketful of Dreams

The bettors, all with a pocketful of dreams, unload on the Derby as on no other race in North America. Consider this: More money was wagered on the 1987 Derby at the track—$6,362,673—than was bet on the entire Derby Day card at the Downs as recently as 1970—$5,811,127. For the ten races held on Derby Day in 1987, a total of $13,576,225 was wagered at the track.

The Derby generates keen betting interest all over the country—in informal office pools as well as at live telecast outlets at other racetracks and off-track betting facilities. In 1987 a total of seventy-three simulcast locations in the United States and Canada held wagering on the Derby, bringing in bets totaling $20,829,236.

For all of the thousands of people across the continent who collect money on the Derby winner, the biggest individual winner of all, of course, is the owner of the victorious horse. In 1978 owner Louis Wolfson told Edward J. McGrath, a Louisville horse-insurance specialist and correspondent for Lloyd's of London, that if Affirmed won the Derby, he wanted the horse's insurance doubled the split second he went under the wire. "When he crossed the finish line, we doubled it right then and there," said McGrath. "I believe it was four to eight [million dollars]." Later, Affirmed was syndicated for $14.4 million, a record at the time.

Living Expenses

As much as the Derby means to the value of a horse, there is only one winner each year, and this business of running racehorses is an expensive proposition for owners, costing an estimated $15,000 to $20,000 annually to maintain a single horse in training at a major racetrack.

Costs vary in different areas, but on the big-time circuits, a trainer alone will charge between $50 and $60 a day for each horse in his care. Veterinary care naturally depends on the health of the horse, but an owner can figure to pay out $3,000 or more a year on the average for such expenses. A horse usually will be reshod once every three weeks, and the cost amounts to more than $50 to $75 for a set of shoes, with patches and other special shoeing extra.

A rule of thumb for transportation costs is $2,500 a year, but for a Kentucky Derby starter the cost is generally higher because a horse of this caliber would be shipped from one track to another to run in stakes races in various locales. Additionally, mortality insurance runs approximately 5 percent of a horse's value.

So an owner has to spend plenty of money to keep a horse at the races. But winning the roses makes it all worthwhile, as evidenced by Alysheba's first-place check of $618,600—a Derby record—for capturing the 1987 renewal.

Roses for Churchill Downs

In terms of a nice-sized profit, Derby weekend has a way of coming up roses for Churchill Downs itself. According to Downs president Tom Meeker, Derby weekend accounts for approximately 17 percent of the track's pari-mutuel handle and 18 percent of attendance for the year. The big weekend also accounts for about 40 percent of the track's gross revenue each year.

A Derby Picnic

The first Derby was a picnic for many racegoers, and local residents sold pralines, fried fish, and chicken from old wicker hampers in the infield. A crowd variously estimated at between 3,000 and 12,000—the figure 10,000 generally is accepted—watched the inaugural Derby, which was a festive

Pari-mutuel machine exhibited in Kentucky Derby Museum

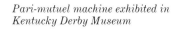

occasion. The Derby has grown to the point at which it is now overwhelming, an awesome occasion whose magnitude can best be told by the numbers supplied by Bill Beam, general manager of the Harry M. Stevens concessions at Churchill Downs.

Mint Julep Mania

"The big item on Derby Day is the mint julep. On Derby Day, 250 vendors sell 80,000 mint juleps in glasses that are redesigned each year. Our recipe calls for 8,000 quarts of Kentucky bourbon with sugar, 60 tons of snow ice, and 150 bushels of fresh mint. Along with that, we sell 7 miles of hot dogs, 4,000 gallons of soda, 1,000 kegs of beer, and 50,000 individual souvenirs. All told on Derby Day, we have about 1,500 employees—about five times our normal work force."

To Beam the Derby means "an all-day celebration. And for a good reason. Everyone knows they will see a tremendous race, good horses, and all the tradition, and they realize that they may see a future Secretariat. Of course, I think everybody dreams of that.

"And then for Kentuckians, in particular, the three big elements of Derby Day are what people of the state are so proud of: beautiful women, great bourbon, and fast horses. It all comes together in a big way on Derby Day."

The engine that drives the horse-racing enterprise is the $2 bet, though if truth be told, a track prefers the $100 bet repeated a thousand times by a few hundred plungers.

Money makes the world go 'round as surely at the track as on Wall Street.

Brought to America from France, the Paris Mutuals System (now pari-mutuels) was used for the first Derby in 1875, along with auction pools in which individual bookmakers ran auctions until they reached a final bid for a horse. Many such pools were created by entrepreneurs who bought the rights from the track, which then stayed clear of wagering.

Auction pools were disbanded in 1889 in answer to a protest by Louisville bookmakers that the pools hurt their business.

In 1978 customers bet over ten million dollars on Derby Day, the first eight-figure handle in the track's history and a long way from the first tabulation of Derby wagering done in 1909. Back then the betting reached $103,694.

Though bettors say they like to make bold plunges, facts show they often like money more than adventure. That much we learn by studying Derby betting history.

Through 1987, favorites won 41 percent of the time. In 113 races, 47 favorites won. So certain (and so cautious) were bettors in 1948 that the entry of Citation and Coaltown paid forty cents on the dollar for Citation's victory.

At every entrance to
Churchill Downs on Derby
Day, men hawk tip sheets
containing suggestions,
information, and, at times, a
plain old guess as to which
horses will run best. These
tip sheets are designed for
the novice who has neither
time nor inclination for
serious study.

The advanced bettor buys the
Daily Racing Form, a digest
of results and entries
compiled by the newspaper's
correspondents.

The Racing Form's
cornucopia of data can
overwhelm a novice. So
many numbers. And what
are those abbreviations so
cryptic as to resemble
hieroglyphics? All is
essential knowledge worth
full concentration. Once the
would-be horseplayer breaks
the Form's code, the world is
at his feet.

There are, certainly, many ways to determine which horse is worth a $2 investment. Some people like to note their hotel room number and use it as guidance for the daily double. Those bettors with a background in fashion often check the day's program for a description of the silks a jockey will wear. Should those silks be a suitable color, the bet is made.

Names of horses are studied, too, with the result that many bets are placed on nags whose only virtue is the lyricism of their birth certificates.

Whatever the method of choice, there must be discipline in the betting, as put best in the immortal words of the Louisville author J. Michael Barry: "I don't expect to win. I just want to lose slowly."

My Old Kentucky Home

t's 4:53 P.M. on the first Saturday in May at Churchill Downs, and the paddock judge is speaking into a microphone from the horse identification office near the paddock. "Bring your horses to the paddock for the eighth race." The eighth race is the Kentucky Derby—and post time is now forty-seven minutes away.

Across the track, far away from the masses that have gathered at rambling Churchill Downs, horsemen are alerted over the public-address system and begin making their way from their barn to the paddock.

The horses have already been bridled, and now the grooms lead them out of their stalls on the back side of the track. The horses' coats are shiny, and some of them have their manes and tails braided. They are all spruced up and ready to go over for the big show.

The Walk to the Paddock

It has been a peaceful day around the barns housing the Derby horses, quite a contrast from what is happening on the other side of the track. In the vicinity of the barns, the atmosphere is calm—so relaxing, in fact, that an hour before the 1977 Derby, the favorite, Seattle Slew, slept. "With all the fanfare, excitement, and crowd, we try to keep him as relaxed as possible," said Billy Turner, the colt's trainer. "This is just like a heavyweight fighter before a championship fight."

For any other race at the Downs the horses head for the paddock individually. For the Derby, the procedure calls for the starters to assemble at the three-quarter-pole gap and come over together. On a normal day at almost any racetrack, not much is made of a horse leaving the stable area for the paddock. But Derby Day at Churchill Downs is not a normal day and racetrackers who otherwise would not bother watching a horse heading to the paddock line up for a close-up glimpse of the Derby field. The Derby entrants that gather at the gap, the twin spires now in full view, walk through a lane of people, many of them photographing the entire lineup of 3-year-olds. Some horses move placidly, seemingly oblivious to the fanfare. Others fling their heads and swish their tails, their rumps bouncing as they walk briskly along.

It is a seven-minute walk from the gap to the paddock. Along the way, each Derby horse receives what is called a bit number from the bit shack, which is located on the outer railing of the turn leading to the clubhouse. This small number, usually hooked to the bit, corresponds to the horse's number and enables fans to identify the starters on their walk to the paddock.

In the past fifteen years or so, a few newsmen have accompanied horses over to the paddock, frequently tagging along with the favorite. Such was the case in 1975 with Foolish Pleasure, who was prancing and waving his head around, looking every bit the part of a colt as ready as possible for the big race. Trainer LeRoy Jolley walked briskly behind Foolish Pleasure along the outside part of the racetrack. Occasionally Jolley would wave or smile at the fans along the fence who shouted out encouragement. But not everybody recognized Foolish Pleasure.

"Who's that?" yelled one spectator.

"Foolish Pleasure," replied the colt's groom.

"Ain't got a prayer!" the fan replied. A foolish opinion, as the talented colt proved within the hour.

In 1977 Seattle Slew, hearing the cheers of the crowd, pricked up his ears and began bouncing. "This is what the Derby's all about," said Billy Turner, the colt's trainer. "This is the moment. When we lead the horse into the paddock, we'll know we've made it to the Derby."

In 1979 trainer Grover "Bud" Delp walked over with Spectacular Bid and yelled out a couple of times to spectators in the clubhouse: "Don't worry about a thing! Go bet!" Those who heeded Bud's advice came away winners.

On his way to the paddock, Spectacular Bid's walk

was delayed by the playing of "The Star-Spangled Banner." Bid's handlers stopped and made a valiant effort to stand at attention while the horse reared and lunged, recalled veteran steward Keene Daingerfield. "I don't know whether Bid's owners were frightened, or even if they saw it, but it terrified the stewards."

The Derby Draws Near

Electricity is in the air as the horses head toward the paddock. The crowd is buzzing, and with the Derby just over a half hour away now, anticipation sweeps the stands.

"There's Alysheba!" they yelled in 1987. "Look at him. Best-looking horse in the race."

The horses walk through the tunnel leading to the paddock. When they reach the end of the tunnel, they are inspected by the horse identifier, who checks the tattoo on the inside of their upper lips. The fans are caught up in the spirit of the day, and while the horse identifier is checking the tattoos, people on both sides of him, from the clubhouse and the grandstand, call out to the horses. The noise is loudest from the grandstand side as exuberant young people come over from the infield as the Derby draws near.

Between 5:06 and 5:08 P.M., the horses arrive at the paddock and enter their stalls to be saddled. While the horses are being saddled, the identifier makes a stop in front of the stalls, checking the colors and markings of each starter, just as he would for any other race.

For the Derbys of 1924 through 1986, the paddock was a close, cramped structure, and frequently horses became upset in the crowded conditions. In 1977 a hectic scene in the paddock caused Seattle Slew to become nervous. The colt kicked a hind leg and hit a board at the rear of his paddock stall. When he appeared on the track for the post parade, he was upset. He had broken out in a sweat and moved along skittishly. "I think the problem was that the paddock was a little bit like a Ringling Brothers circus," said Mickey Taylor, the thirty-

two-year-old part-owner of Seattle Slew. "Every person we ever met wanted to shake hands in the [paddock] stall."

Churchill Downs built a new paddock for the fall meeting of 1986, and this facility is roomier and safer for the traditionally large Derby fields and paddock visitors.

Thirty minutes before post time the jockeys begin stepping on the scale in the second-floor jockeys' quarters, and the clerk of scales checks each rider to make sure that his or her weight, with tack, is 126 pounds (121 for those riding fillies). Twenty minutes before post time, the waiting ends for the Derby jockeys, and the clerk sends them to the paddock, their silks glistening brightly.

In 1929 Derby starter Clyde Van Dusen was so small that his trainer, after whom the horse was named, made it a point to go to the jockeys' quarters before the Derby and tell his rider, Linus "Pony" McAtee, who had never seen the mount, not to be discouraged by the horse's size. "He can't be small enough to surprise me," McAtee assured Van Dusen. "I've ridden some mighty little horses." Even though forewarned, McAtee was shocked when he came to the paddock and had his first glimpse of Clyde Van Dusen, who at 900 pounds was outweighed by some opponents by more than 200 pounds. Clyde Van Dusen was tiny, but McAtee soon learned that he was all racehorse. "He's just a pony," McAtee exclaimed after Clyde Van Dusen splattered through deep mud to win. "But he's the sweetest package of thoroughbred horseflesh I ever rode."

Riders Up!

By 5:15 P.M. or so the horses are saddled, and a few minutes afterward the trainers are talking to their jockeys.

"Riders up!" announces the paddock judge at 5:19 P.M. The trainers give their jockeys a leg up, and it is time for the horses to head back through the tunnel on their way to the track. With the playing of "My Old Kentucky Home," many fans

The Track at Churchill Downs

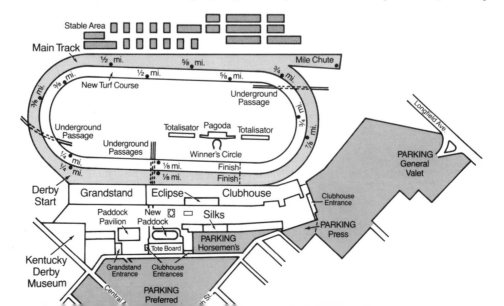

begin to become misty-eyed; there is no question this is one of the most emotional of moments in sports.

Back in 1925, however, it was rain, not tears, that rolled down the faces of the crowd as the horses left the paddock. A storm hit shortly before the Derby, and once the rains came, women hurried for shelter. A number did not reach safety in time, though, and many crepe gowns and lace-trimmed hats were ruined.

The late Frank Coltiletti, who rode Voltaic in the '25 Derby, never forgot the way the rain slanted down from the skies that afternoon. "Just when we was comin' out of the paddock, a big rainstorm hit," he recalled. "You'd think the end of the world arrived. As we were walking out under the archway leading to the track, the downpour was so fierce that you couldn't see your hand in front of you. And that made it good for Flying Ebony, who loved mud."

The 1925 renewal was the fifth of seven races on the card, and the Derby's post time was about an hour earlier than it is today. Nowadays the eighth of ten races on the card, the Derby has a 5:40 post time, and at approximately 5:25 the horses enter the track.

It is believed that "My Old Kentucky Home" was played during the Derby's post parade for the first time in 1930. Everybody stands now, more than 130,000 fans, as the sleek, finely tuned thoroughbreds come out from the tunnel and step onto the track.

Virtually every horse is escorted by a rider aboard a "pony," actually a full-grown horse. In the old days, ponies rarely accompanied horses to the gate. Riders were expected to be able to take care of their horses without them. But times have changed, and now trainers feel that a pony helps riders conserve their energy for the race. Trainers hire the riders of these ponies, many of whom go from track to track and "pony" horses exclusively. These pony riders also help to calm horses during the parade to the post. If a horse becomes rank, the jockey can count on the assistance of a pony rider instead of struggling himself with an unruly horse.

The horses continue to come out of the paddock as the field heads down the track toward the clubhouse turn. Sometimes, if the field is large, the playing of "My Old Kentucky Home" is finished even before the last horse comes onto the track. As the song ends the crowd cheers, and soon the horses canter up the track. The Derby is about ten minutes away, and the jockeys are warming up their horses. Soon it is time for them to be loaded into the starting gate. Assistant starters, usually one per Derby horse, lead the horses into the gate. The assistant then climbs into the starting gate stall, to hold his horse's head straight in these final seconds.

Official Viewers

All officials are in place. Up in the stewards' stand, two of the judges are outside, looking through their binoculars, waiting for the start. Inside the stewards' room, the third judge is prepared to observe the Derby on two television monitors, one showing a head-on view and the other the pan or side view. Also available, essentially as a backup, is another TV monitor with ABC's national telecast of the Derby.

After the race, all three stewards will gather to watch replays of the Derby from the different cameras. Their objective is to look for interference in the race. Only once in the Derby's history has a horse been disqualified as a result of such an incident; in 1984 Gate Dancer finished fourth but was disqualified and placed fifth for lugging in and bumping Fali Time several times in the homestretch.

In 1968 another type of incident led to the disqualification of Dancer's Image as the Derby winner. Medication, then illegal but now permissible, was found in his system, and after lengthy legal proceedings, he ultimately was stripped of his Derby victory. Forward Pass, the second-place finisher, was subsequently recognized as the winner of that race.

The stewards are not the only officials keeping a close eye on the Derby. Three patrol judges are in their stands, one near the five-eighths pole, another close to the three-eighths pole, and one just past the finish line. It is their job to watch for infractions during the race. Immediately after the race, they converse with the stewards.

Starter Tom Wagoner is in his stand, ready to send the field on its way. As the last horse moves into the gate, the jockeys are all concentrating, anticipating the start. Upstairs in the announcer's booth, Mike Battaglia calls out, "It is now post time."

Wagoner observes that all starters are standing with their heads straight ahead. The time is 5:40 P.M. Wagoner does not waste a moment. He presses a button, and it is a perfect start.

They're off and running in the Kentucky Derby.

They were born for this first Saturday in May when they walk to the post for the greatest horse race in the world. These are babies, only 3 years old, not yet as strong as they will be, not yet as fast. But on the first Saturday in May of a colt's third year he learns what he's made of, for then he runs the longest race of his life against the best colts of his crop. If he has what the hardboots call "heart," if he refuses to be beaten, the Derby will be the evidence. This is his chance of a lifetime.

Of the tens of thousands of foals born each spring, no more than twenty make it to the Derby. They can come from million-dollar stables with a dozen trainers, a hundred grooms, and a full support team including veterinarians and nutritionists. They may move from track to track by private jet. Yet all this is rendered meaningless if the colt so much as has a bellyache. If he gets rambunctious, as all thoroughbreds do, he may just kick the side of his stall, and that quickly he can be injured and out of the race for which he has been bred and trained.

No second chances in the lifetime of a Derby horse. He's 3 years old only once. Only once can he follow the lead ponies into the post parade for the Kentucky Derby.

Less than three years ago this colt trotted alongside his mother in a pasture. Then the dream was only beginning, then every colt had a chance. Old men live a lifetime of dreams, and horses are born to the dream, born to run. Poetry becomes bone and muscle. They danced in the meadows as yearlings, came to the bridle eager, took a rider's first weight in a stall, and walked to a starting gate as if born to the moment.

One chance.

One chance only.

After they leave the barn area on the walk to the paddock for saddling, the horses' handlers pick up identifying numbers that match the saddlecloths. This number is clipped to the bit only until the horse reaches the paddock entrance.

Every ribbon and flower is in place on the lead pony when it's time to begin the walk from the backstretch and on toward the paddock.

It's a seven-minute walk with your horse on a shank. As you move, you do not so much hear the crowd's boisterous noise as feel it, a steady, thundering vibration against your chest.

Entering the tunnel, the horses disappear from the view of the 100,000-plus folks in the grandstand and infield. Just a minute away owners are waiting in the paddock. Here in 1979, with Spectacular Bid, trainer Bud Delp shouted to front-row customers, "Go bet!"

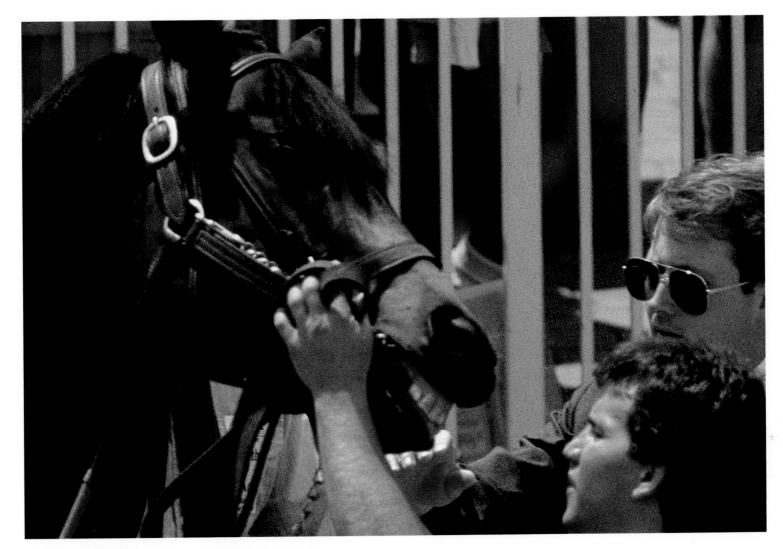

To be certain this Derby horse is who he's claimed to be, a racing official checks his lip tattoo.

A safeguard against "ringers," or horses running under assumed names, tattoos usually are applied when a horse first races at a track. The Thoroughbred Racing Protection Bureau does the marking. The tattoo is two parts—a letter indicating the year of foaling and a number matching the registration number of the Jockey Club foal certificate.

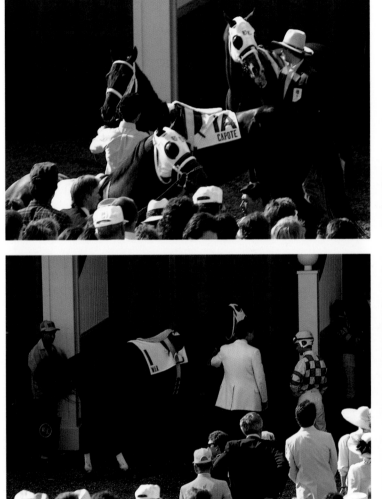

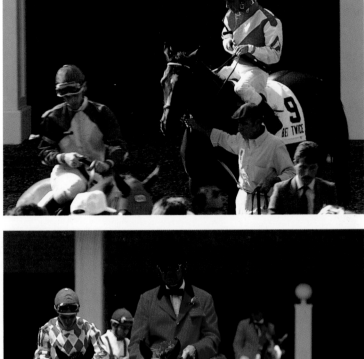

The call to the post, a single brass horn in the Churchill Downs presentation stand, has a startling effect on the crowd. It brings silence that in the next moment becomes a roar of expectation, for now the horses will come back from the paddock and onto the track in full view again for the parade to the post.

In the paddock, the horses are saddled and walking. The race is perhaps ten minutes away. Time moves slowly now. The vise of time has been closing on the trainer and jockey for months. Today they meet in the paddock. There's not much to say. A word, a sentence. No great strategy now. They know what the horse can do. What they need now is the luck of the race. A hole on the rail, maybe, and time to get through before it closes.

A voice calls, "Riders up!" Trainers give a leg-up to the little men who sit high on the big horses. Once separate beings, they are now fused— a single entity of great beauty. In one minute, walking through the paddock tunnel into sunlight, they'll hear racing's most famous song, "My Old Kentucky Home."

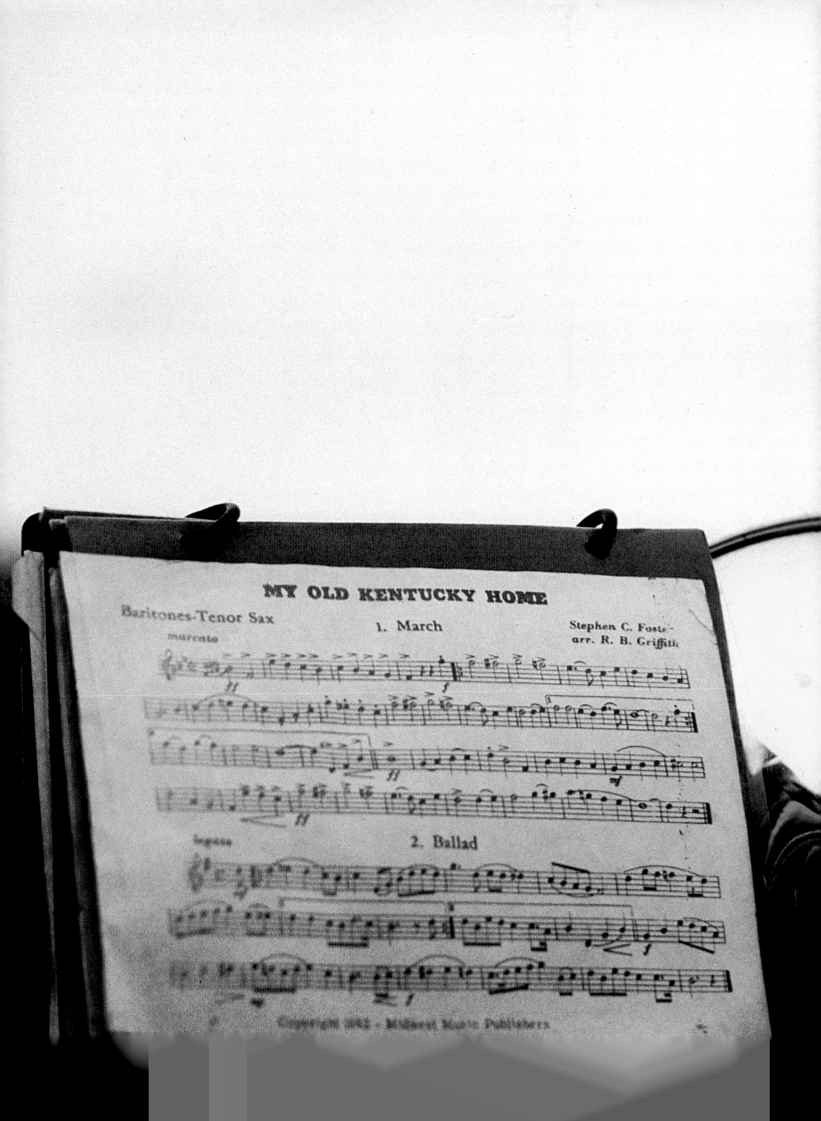

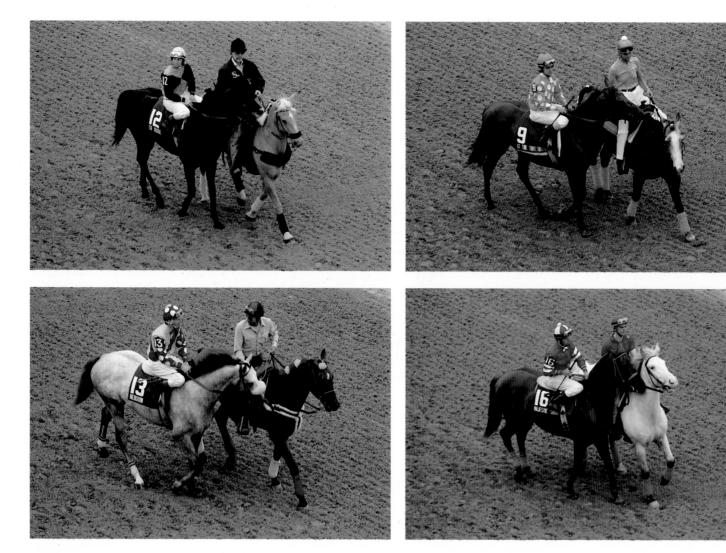

They have come from the paddock-tunnel darkness to parade in the dazzle of day, all the Derby horses in a row walking past the grandstand. Even walking they seem to fly, moving with an airy strut that is mesmerizing in its grace and power.

They have warmed up with slow turns on the backside, and now are walking again toward the starting gate.

The rider knows more about his horse now than he did fifteen minutes ago. He can feel the muscles and he knows what each movement means.

Not long ago, two summers only, the colt first felt a man's weight on his back and walked toward a steel contraption foreign to his experience. Soon enough, he stood in the tight space of a gate stall. And they shut the door in front of him the second week.

They once started the Derby with a whip cracking against horses held behind a webbing stretched across the track.

Now, the starter rolls a steel gate across the track by the quarter-pole at the top of the Churchill Downs stretch. The horses will pass here twice, once leaving the gate and again with a quarter-mile to run down a stretch some call Heartbreak Lane.

With only a minute to post time, the assistant starter will guide the horses into their numbered stalls.

Run for the Roses

Racing has a variety of strategies. Some trainers use a "rabbit" to tire the pacesetters and set the race up for a come-from-behind charge by a stablemate. Others instruct their jockeys to go to the front and try to conserve the horse as much as possible. Some jockeys lay just off the pace or stay somewhere in the middle of the pack, patiently waiting to make their move at the opportune time, while others plan to surge from far back near the end of the race. The come-from-behind strategy usually needs two elements to succeed: a swift pace in front to soften up the leaders and good racing luck in avoiding traffic jams.

Using a Rabbit

A rabbit—Aristides—was used in the inaugural Kentucky Derby of 1875. Price McGrath, who owned Aristides, planned that the colt would serve only one purpose in the Derby: to ensure a rapid pace. The intention was that the early leaders would tire and would be passed by Aristides' more heralded stablemate, Chesapeake, who would rally to victory in the stretch.

As the race unfolded, Volcano and McCreery dueled immediately for the lead, followed closely by Verdigris and Aristides, while the sluggish Chesapeake lagged behind. McCreery, setting a blistering pace, led the field past the grandstand the first time. The field of fifteen thundered around the clubhouse turn, and then McCreery suddenly tired. Aristides moved swiftly to take over the lead.

Making sure that the pace would remain a torrid one, jockey Oliver Lewis pushed Aristides on as he raced down the backstretch. Approaching the far turn, Lewis then began to ease up on his mount, a clear indication that he thought his mission was accomplished. According to the game plan, it was now time for Chesapeake to come on.

As the field began to straighten out for home, McGrath was puzzled. He tried to spot Chesapeake, who was nowhere to be found among the front-runners, but little Aristides was still up there in the lead, running his heart out. Lewis looked over at McGrath standing at trackside, for some kind of signal. "Go on!" shouted McGrath.

Lewis then loosened his pull on Aristides' reins and drove the colt down the stretch. Although Volcano made a bid in midstretch, Aristides had enough left in reserve to streak under the wire two lengths ahead. Chesapeake, the Derby favorite, was eighth in a cloud of dust.

A Waiting Game

Patience is an all-important quality for Derby jockeys, but it is a virtue that historically has been lacking in all too many. Braulio Baeza is an example of a jockey who went to the front too soon one year, then patiently waited the next to win the roses. In the 1962 Derby, Baeza, on Admiral's Voyage, held the lead after a mile in 1:35⅕, then the fastest clocking for that distance in Derby history. Admiral's Voyage wound up finishing ninth. The following year, Baeza had the mount on Chateaugay, who was sixth after six furlongs in a then record 1:10 for the Derby's first three-quarters of a mile. Chateaugay then moved up to fourth after a mile in 1:35⅖. After such a fast pace, the leaders were exhausted in the stretch, and Chateaugay overtook them all to carry Baeza to a 1¼-length victory.

In contrast to the rushing tactics of many jockeys, the 1891 Derby featured a waiting game played by all four jockeys in the race. They held back for such a long time that the race looked as if it were being run in slow motion. Finally, at the head of the stretch, the horses were put into a drive. Isaac Murphy managed to get Kingman home first in the horse-and-buggy clocking of 2:52¼, almost eighteen seconds slower than the Derby record for the race's $1\frac{1}{2}$-mile distance of that time. Afterward, the 1891 renewal was dubbed "The Funeral Procession."

Nobody ever used better judgment in more Derbys than Bill Hartack. He was at his best in the Derbys, winning five times to tie Eddie Arcaro for the all-time record. None of Hartack's winners ever led the Derby early. At the start of the long Churchill Downs homestretch, Hartack wanted his horses to have something left for the final grueling quarter of a mile.

Front-Runners

Speed can be dangerous in any race, but a front-running style has often paid off in the Run for the Roses. From 1909 through 1912, each Derby winner led all, or virtually all, of the way. Sir Barton, the first Triple Crown winner (1919), led at every call of his Derby victory, as did another Triple Crown king, Count Fleet (1943). Other recent Derby winners who have shown a good lick of speed in the early going include Dark Star (1953), Swaps (1955), Kauai King (1966), Riva Ridge (1972), Bold Forbes (1976), and Spend a Buck (1985).

In 1985 Spend a Buck inherited the lead by default after Eternal Prince, who was expected to hook up with him in an early speed duel, got off to a bad start. Spend a Buck's jockey, Angel Cordero, Jr., repeated the wire-to-wire strategy that had made him the winner of the 1976 Derby aboard Bold Forbes, another colt gifted with speed. Spend a Buck led through six furlongs in 1:09$\frac{3}{5}$ and a mile in 1:34$\frac{4}{5}$, the fastest fractions for those distances in Derby history. Normally, a horse would wilt after such a demanding pace, but not Spend a Buck. He was far ahead and running unchallenged in the lead, and there was no catching him coming down the stretch. He hit the wire $5\frac{1}{4}$ lengths in front in a remarkable performance.

Traffic Jams

Generally, a horse cannot have it both ways, running fast early and having something left for the end. The fastest opening quarter (:21$\frac{4}{5}$) and first half-mile (:45$\frac{1}{5}$) in Derby history were achieved by Top Avenger in the 1981 race. He wound up finishing an exhausted nineteenth. The pace was so swift that the race was set up for a come-from-behind victory—and that is what Pleasant Colony did, rallying from seventeenth place. He managed to avoid the traffic jams, unlike Woodchopper.

Woodchopper, next to last under Eddie Delahoussaye the first time under the wire, was trapped when the cumbersome field hit the top of the stretch. He finally got out of the heavy traffic as he approached the three-sixteenths pole. Eighth at that time, he proceeded to sail past horses, and even though jockey Jorge Velasquez might have been taking it easy on Pleasant Colony near the finish, Woodchopper's surge was impressive as he closed to finish second, beaten by only three-quarters of a length.

Woodchopper went on to run dull races in the next two legs of the Triple Crown, finishing eleventh in the Preakness and fourth in the Belmont. But seven years earlier, Little Current, another horse who had encountered traffic problems in the Derby, had come back to win the Preakness and Belmont.

Little Current finished fifth in the crowded 1974 Derby, which drew a record twenty-three starters for the centennial running of the race. His overall problems in the Derby, though serious, were not well publicized. Bobby Ussery, who rode Little Current in the Derby, complained afterward about the traffic. But with so many other jockeys complaining, Ussery's comments were overlooked. On the day of the Preakness, however, his observations were verified when stop-action films of the Derby showed a nationwide audience all the trouble Little Current had experienced.

Under jockey Mike Rivera, Little Current went on to win both the Preakness and Belmont by the same margin—seven lengths—en route to capturing the Eclipse Award as the champion 3-year-old colt. But for the Derby's traffic problems he might have been a Triple Crown winner, and after the 1974 Derby,

1/4 mile

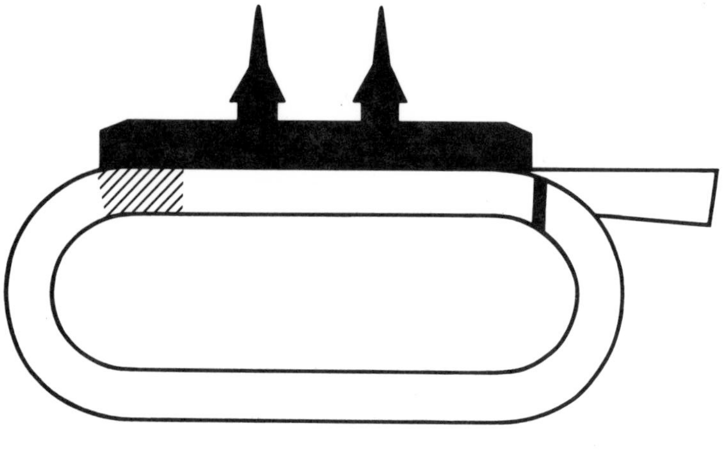

1/2 mile

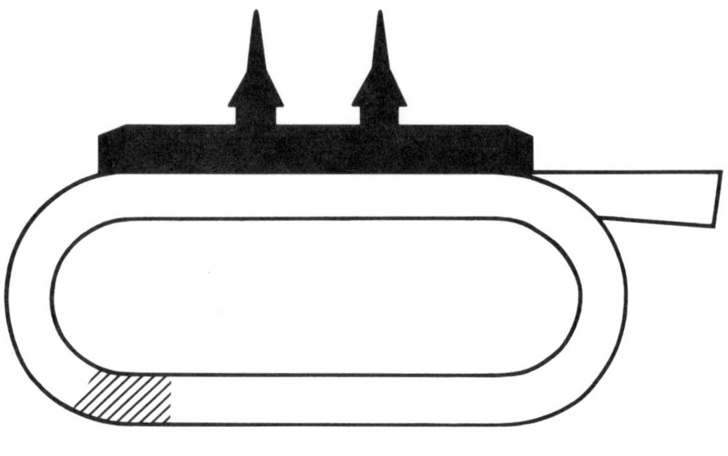

Churchill Downs began limiting the race to twenty starters.

Late Charges

Though Little Current and Woodchopper were thwarted in their come-from-behind charges, some horses have successfully rallied from far back in the Derby. Besides Pleasant Colony, modern-day horses who made up a lot of ground to win the roses include Ponder, Needles, Carry Back, Secretariat, Gato Del Sol, and Ferdinand.

Carry Back's late charge was one of the most memorable in Derby history. Announcer Bryan Field did not give Carry Back, the favorite, much of a chance as the horses swept into the stretch in the 1961 Derby.

"Carry Back is far out of it at this stage . . . into the stretch, it is still Globemaster, Four-and-Twenty, and Crozier ranging up on the outside, a three-horse battle. Carry Back is too far back to make it . . . can't unless he hurries. . . ."

Could Carry Back, ridden by Johnny Sellers, make it? With a quarter of a mile to go, he trailed the leader by more than thirteen lengths, more than one-third the length of a football field. Small wonder that many of Carry Back's supporters had given up hope. At this stage of the race, even Carry Back's trainer and breeder, Jack Price, did not think his colt would win.

Down the stretch they charged. The leaders were beginning to tire. And here came Carry Back, the courageous colt charging past the faltering front-runners one by one. Crozier, meanwhile, made a move for the lead under jockey Braulio Baeza. "I'm passing Four-and-Twenty," Baeza later recalled, "but I see this horse coming up on the outside. Can only be one. Carry Back."

Carry Back was fourth at the stretch call, and inside the eighth pole he surged to third place—then to second place. Now only Crozier was left to be caught.

History has shown that the Derby winner usually has the lead at the eighth pole. Only occasionally does a horse come through with a closing burst in the final furlong to win the roses. Now inside the eighth pole, Crozier was desperately trying to hang on, and Carry Back was fighting to catch him. Field told the spellbound audience: "Crozier now on the outside in front. Crozier in the lead, and it looks for sure that Globemaster is beaten and so is Four-and-Twenty. And here comes Carry Back, the favorite. Carry Back after Crozier. Crozier with a chance to turn the tables, Carry Back charging! Carry Back coming! Carry Back in front. Carry Back's gonna win! Here's the finish—Carry Back by three-quarters! Crozier is second . . . ."

Roughriders

Saving as much ground as possible is a sound strategy in any race, but in the 1928 Derby jockey Chick Lang deliberately took a circuitous route aboard the victorious Reigh Count. Jockey Willie Garner, who finished second aboard Misstep in that race, recalled the strategy employed by the Reigh Count camp.

"I knew that Reigh Count was the horse to beat," Garner said. "I was in front all the way, and I was hoping Reigh Count would get into some trouble. But I looked up at the head of the stretch, and here comes Reigh Count. So I figured I'd do everything I could to him."

Those were the roughriding days, before the patrol film. "In those days, you could do anything you wanted," Garner said. "So whatever I could have done, I done it and got by with it. I could have either grabbed his saddlecloth or bumped him or something."

As he learned later, Reigh Count's trainer, Bert Michell, had warned Chick Lang that whatever he did, he was not to get close to Garner. "So he come 'way wide and went around me and beat me," Garner said.

Overcoming Trouble

The unexpected always happens in a race—a bad start or heavy traffic problems—and seasoned

Backstretch

Finish

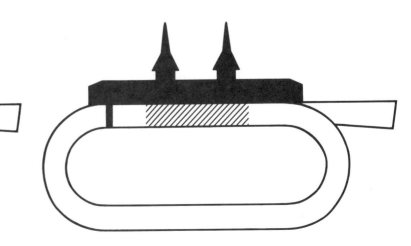

jockeys are able to react and adjust quickly to varied situations.

In the '77 Derby, Jean Cruguet on Seattle Slew got off to a nearly disastrous start, swerving to his right as he came out of the gate from the number 4 post position. He was behind a wall of horses, and his backers gasped. After being jarred slightly off balance in the saddle, Cruguet then began the work of getting Seattle Slew back into the Derby.

Seattle Slew charged his way through the field so rapidly that as he passed the wire for the first time, he was right alongside the leader, For The Moment. The time for the opening quarter was :23 flat. The two raced together, with For The Moment holding a head lead over Seattle Slew after a brisk half-mile in :45⅘.

Swinging around the far turn, Seattle Slew came up to challenge For The Moment. It was a two-horse battle rounding the turn, and when they hit the top of the stretch, Seattle Slew had put away For The Moment and taken the lead. With Cruguet applying the whip, Seattle Slew moved to a three-length advantage at the eighth pole.

Run Dusty Run and Sanhedrin were rallying from behind, but it was too late for them. At the finish it was Seattle Slew by a length and three-quarters over Run Dusty Run, who finished a neck in front of Sanhedrin. For The Moment dropped back to eighth.

This race made a deep impression on many observers, more than a few of whom thought it was one of the greatest performances in the Derby's history. After getting off to that bad start, Seattle Slew demonstrated his genuine ability by hurrying into contention, putting away the speed, and then holding off the come-from-behind horses.

He was truly a great horse, that Seattle Slew.

Late on the first Saturday afternoon in May the kaleidoscope is turned one last time, transforming the day's images—so dazzling in color and shape—into a single, narrowly focused piece. No longer are we concerned with the periphery. Our eyes have scanned the length and breadth of the spectacle. Stored away are the sights in the vault of our memory bank reserved for life's fascinations.

At 5:40 P.M., we hear the track announcer call: "It is now post time!"

For any race anywhere, those words carry the thrill of questions about to be answered. Everything before—long nights of worry, bright mornings of hope—is forgotten in favor of what is to come. The verdict can be rendered so quickly that we don't know what happened or why. The value of years of work will be determined in two minutes.

At post time all eyes turn to the starting gate and lock onto the steel cages, which on this Saturday in May of 1987 wait for seventeen starters. For the man in charge of loading the horses into the gate and starting the race fairly, the moment is charged with a drama that passes unnoticed. His work and that of assistants handling the horses is done with such directness it seems routine. Yet their work can be not only dangerous but decisive in the running of the race. It may take four men to persuade a colt to enter the gate. Other men stand astride the stall walls, there to keep the waiting horses calm while the rest are loaded, a chore that might take two minutes.

Only when all the horses are standing straight does the starter press the button. The gate doors explode open.

This is not the only sound. A bell rings loudly the length of the gate. The morning's silence becomes the afternoon's clamor.

Fans of all stripes come to the Derby from little burgs and cosmopolitan cities here and around the world. Not all bring binoculars, but those who do are real horseplayers.

With binoculars, the tiny and distant images are brought near so that a horseplayer can study his investment at a thousand yards. Did the colt get so excited by the crowd's noise that he broke into a nervous lather? Did he warm up well? Is the rider sitting comfortably?

Trainers cherish binoculars as if they are religious artifacts, without which a man's passage to heaven cannot be guaranteed.

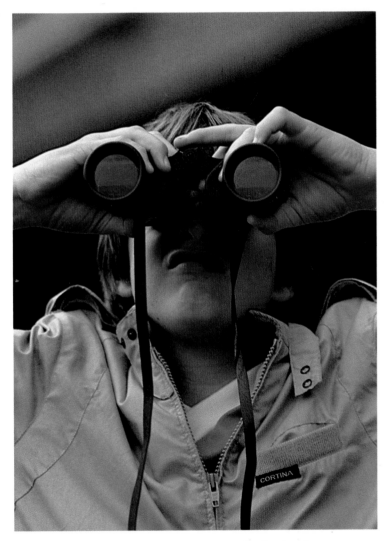

"My eyes," Woody Stephens calls his binoculars, and he carries a case of such ancient manufacture that the leather is scuffed up into tiny balls of time.

"If I didn't have these glasses," Stephens says, "I'd go plumb crazy 'cause I'd never see my horses 'cept in the barn, and they don't ever win no money in the barn."

Not only do the glasses serve a physical function, they bring the horseplayer's mind to the sharp concentration that is distinctive of tunnel vision. The world becomes a smaller place, its boundaries set by the rims of the binoculars.

The horses parade past the grandstand and walk to the track's backside, each step taken under the careful gaze of distant horseplayers holding glasses focused on them. On the backstretch, when the horses gallop to warm up, binoculars follow them. Then, at last, all glasses turn toward the starting gate with the seventeen Derby horses. It is 5:40 P.M.—post time!

Seventeen horses are locked in the gate, ready to run the Derby's mile and a quarter. From the white pillar at the track's edge, it is a quarter mile down the homestretch to the finish line. But the first time past it's not the "finish" line, since the colts must still circle the track. It's a mile before reaching this white pole again. At that point, they'll have the same quarter-mile to run—only this time they'll be a quarter-mile from winning the race of a lifetime.

As the gates spring open, a horse's first move is not to run but to jump, pushing off with his hind legs. The noise of the clattering gates and clanging bells is joined by raucous whoops from the jockeys.

Conventional wisdom insisted for years that the best route down the stretch the first time was a path that took the horse to the rail quickly, and then allowed him to straighten out for the run to the clubhouse turn.

Arthur B. Hancock III decided in 1982 that geometry dictated a new course. His horse, Gato Del Sol, from the eighteenth post position, would run as straight as possible to the turn, in effect tracing the long side of an isosceles triangle. Perhaps the few feet saved by such triangulation were vital. Gato Del Sol won easily.

Two jumps out of the gate, whips in hand to crack their horses once, jockeys are rocked back in the stirrups. Now for the long run. Now each jockey falls into rhythm with his horse. They look for room in the traffic, a fast way back to the quarter-pole, a lifetime away.

Because so many horses of comparable ability run in it, the Derby often is a stampede of a race. Coming to the seven-sixteenths pole in the 1987 running, the field is tightly bunched.

Bending around the far turn, On the Line (in white blinkers) leads as Bet Twice moves up alongside in a run that promises the race is his.

Not even through the first turn, Laffit Pincay, Jr., on Masterful Advocate is bumped against the rail. War "almost went over the rail in the first turn," his jockey, Herb McCauley, says later. Leaving these colts far behind, along with the favorite, Demons Begone, who is pulled up when he bleeds from the nose, the field charges onward.

They've run the better part of a mile by now, and every rider knows how much longer and faster his horse can run. But race strategy depends on unforeseeable events. No one plans on being shoved against the rail. No one knows when horses will move aside and give those behind room to run.

Bumped coming out of the gate and squeezed back to fourteenth in the field, McCarron and Alysheba move to the rail and stay there around the first turn. Alysheba runs on the outside as he heads down the backstretch, passing a dozen horses until only a stride separates him from the leaders.

A Derby horse is bred to run and a trainer teaches him how. But in the end it's the jockey who finds the fastest way to the wire. Somewhere in this crush rides Chris McCarron on Alysheba.

Four abreast, the leaders gallop past the seven-sixteenths pole, with On the Line on the rail, Bet Twice alongside him, then Avie's Copy running next to Alysheba.

It's a run to the wire—the test is not so much of a rider's cunning but more of a horse's stamina and heart. No more turns in heavy traffic, no more jostling for position. Now the race is simple. Or so it seems.

Bet Twice (No. 9) takes the lead rounding off the final turn as On the Line fades and Alysheba moves strongly on the outside. Soon it will be Bet Twice on the rail with Alysheba under McCarron's whip as they move into the unforgettable stretch run.

253

A quarter-mile long, the stretch at Churchill Downs is known as Heartbreak Lane because so many dreams are shattered there. Before 1987, though, the Derby winner had led at the eighth pole for eleven straight years and eighteen out of nineteen. So when Bet Twice takes the lead at the quarter-pole and holds it inside the eighth pole, he looks a sure winner.

Victory seems even more certain when Alysheba, running second, clips Bet Twice's heels and nearly stumbles.

Alysheba's head whips forward, almost to the ground. He seems about to skid to his knees in a frightful prelude to the calamity of horses falling over horses. Yet somehow, Alysheba regains his balance and moves up on Bet Twice.

"Heart," trainer Jack Van Berg says afterwards. "He kept his feet because he's got a great heart."

Bet Twice's rider, Craig Perret, never sees Alysheba behind him, never feels Alysheba's hoof strike against his horse because Bet Twice has swerved right in the stretch—into Alysheba's path. They have only twenty more seconds to run. Perret has a race to win, so there is no looking back. After the race, Perret says: "I straightened my horse up and he went on and ran. If there was contact, I couldn't tell."

McCarron lurches forward onto Alysheba's neck as he stumbles. Afterward he remembers, "I thought I was gone."

Bet Twice still leads with a sixteenth of a mile to go, another six or seven seconds to run, six or seven seconds to a dream. But here comes Alysheba at full tilt after regaining his balance with three-sixteenths of a mile to go. Side by side. Stride for stride. The 100,000-plus fans are aflame with the moment's passion.

Alysheba's performance is amazing, from being bumped at the start and shuffled back to fourteenth in a seventeen-horse field and forced to run wide on the last turn, he then nearly trips in the stretch. Still he passes Bet Twice inside the sixteenth pole. With seventy yards to go, McCarron screams, "C'mon, wire!"

The Sweet Smell of Success

One of the finest jockeys the country ever produced, Isaac Burns Murphy was born during the Civil War, when men of his color were second-class citizens. He became one of the most respected and celebrated figures on the American turf in the nineteenth century. Murphy not only rode the winners of three Kentucky Derbys—Buchanan in 1884, Riley in 1890, and Kingman in 1891—but his lifetime average of 44 percent winners, based on 628 victories from 1,412 mounts between 1875 and 1895, remains the highest on record.

A Man of Honor

It was as a gentleman and a paragon of honesty that Murphy earned a reputation unique among jockeys of his day. His integrity in the face of endless temptation was widely known and admired. His fame has endured the ages. In 1955, when the first elections were held for the Racing Hall of Fame in the National Museum of Racing at Saratoga, Murphy was elected by a landslide vote of a nationwide panel of racing writers.

A Bad Actor

Murphy had his first Kentucky Derby victory on Buchanan in 1884. Owned by William Cottrill and trained by William Bird, Buchanan was a talented rogue. He could run but was obstreperous. He had failed to win in six starts at 2, but had finished second five times.

That spring Murphy, in a weak moment, accepted the mount. But Buchanan was such a bad actor that Murphy wanted no part of him for the tenth Kentucky Derby and told Bird to get another jockey. Bird went to the stewards, who told Murphy he had to ride or he would be suspended. Murphy reluctantly mounted the horse, who promptly was fractious at the post, delaying the start. Buchanan got away poorly, but Murphy, with patience and firmness, got him to settle in stride and save ground along the rail. Moving to the outside on the turn for racing room, Murphy set Buchanan down for the drive and the colt responded, winning by a length.

Back-to-Back Derbys

Murphy had his second Kentucky Derby victory aboard Ed Corrigan's Riley in 1890. Riley had been a useful 2-year-old for owner-trainer Corrigan, winning six of twelve starts, but Robespierre was the horse to beat in the 16th Derby and went off at even money. Robespierre was the early leader, but gradually Murphy improved his position with Riley, took command at the head of the stretch, and won by a length and three quarters at odds of 4–1.

Only four jockeys have won back-to-back Derbys. They are Jimmy Winkfield, another black rider, who won in 1901 and 1902 with His Eminence and Alan-a-Dale; Ron Turcotte, who won in 1972 and 1973 with Riva Ridge and Secretariat; Eddie Delahoussaye, who won in 1982 and 1983 with Gato Del Sol and Sunny's Halo; and Murphy, who followed his 1890 victory aboard Riley with a win on Kingman in 1891.

The first twenty-one Kentucky Derbys were contested at the traditional English classic distance of a mile and a half. Yet American racing men were always more enamored of speed than stamina, and when the Kentucky Derby began drawing smaller and smaller fields, Churchill Downs cut the distance to a mile and a quarter in 1896.

One of the races that prompted this decision was the 1891 running, which drew only four 3-year-olds. The race is distinguished to this day as the slowest Derby ever run and probably the weirdest. After the first quarter-mile the horses traveled like cavalry, side by side, each jockey waiting for the other to set the pace. Finally, Murphy "sent" Kingman, and the bay colt won by half a length over Balgowan in the leisurely time of 2:52¼. A respectable time would have been 2:37. Kingman had been heavily favored, so form held up, to the delight of the large crowd.

Last Rides

Murphy rode in the Kentucky Derby of 1893 but could fare no better than fifth with Mirage, who showed early speed and tired.

Faced with difficulties staying at racing weight and with his health compromised, Murphy rode little in 1894 and had his last ride in the fall of 1895 in Lexington. Murphy's mount, Tupta, a notorious quitter in most of his races, won that day.

The following winter Murphy took ill, and he was dead at thirty-five. He was a legend in his time, and his fame today is greater than ever. Thousands view his grave each year at the Kentucky Horse Park near Lexington.

The Ruler of Racing

In the Roaring Twenties the Ruler of Racing was jockey Earl Sande, whose 968 victories from 3,673 mounts gave him a remarkably high career-winning-average of 26 percent. By comparison, Bill Shoemaker's average is 22.4 percent, Eddie Arcaro's was 20 percent, Johnny Longden's was 19 percent, and Angel Cordero, Jr.'s, is 18 percent. Like Murphy, Sande also rode three Kentucky Derby winners. Only three other riders have won more Derbys.

Sande also had five winners of the Belmont Stakes as well as five winners of the Jockey Club Gold Cup. He was a standout of his time, and although he rode against such aces as Laverne Fator, Carroll Schilling, and Buddy Ensor, it was Sande who was the hero of "The Handy Guy" poems by the journalist Damon Runyon, who captured the Guys and Dolls flavor of racing so well.

Riding for the Rancocas Stable of oil man Harry Sinclair, Sande was America's leading money-winning rider in 1921 and again in 1923, the season he set a record for purses of $569,394 that was to stand for twenty years. That was also the year he won his first Kentucky Derby with the Rancocas colt Zev, trained by the famed Missouri horseman Sam Hildreth.

Zev was a useful 2-year-old of 1922, winning five of twelve starts. Over the winter Hildreth freshened him and Zev came out as a 3-year-old in smashing fashion to beat older horses in the Paumonk Handicap at Jamaica. Zev also won the Rainbow Handicap but in the Preakness finished a very disappointing twelfth position in a field of thirteen.

It was Sande who persuaded Sinclair and Hildreth that Zev should have a chance to redeem himself by running in the 49th Derby. In the large field of twenty-one, Zev went off at 19–1. Hildreth, like the public, did not think much of his colt's chances and sent his assistant to Louisville to saddle the colt.

The public considered Zev a sprinter and Sande agreed that speed was the colt's strong suit. He put Zev on the lead shortly after the start and kept him there to score by a length and a half.

The Handy Guy

Sande got his second Derby victory in 1925, more or less by accident. He had a brilliant season in 1923, with a record thirty-nine stakes victories. However, in 1924 a nasty spill and a subsequent gallstone operation kept him on the sidelines for eight months.

When he returned to action, in 1925, he had difficulty obtaining good mounts. The Derby that year, the first broadcast on radio, was wide open, with a twenty-horse field. Flying Ebony, a black colt by The Finn who was trained by W.B. Duke, was part of the mutuel field.

Several riders had been on Flying Ebony, who had won four of eight starts at 2 without distinguishing himself. He had failed to show much at the start of his 3-year-old season, and his owner, Gifford Cochran, was undecided about starting him in the Derby. Friends persuaded him to run his horse and to use Sande.

Maybe there'll be another,
Heady and game, an' true—
Maybe we'll find his brother
a-drivin' them horses thru.
Maybe—but, say, I doubt it,
Never his like again—
Never a handy
Guy like Sande,
Bootin' them babies in.

Green an' white at the quarter—
Say, I can see him now,
Ratin' them just as he orter,
Workin' them up—an' how.
Green an' white at the homestretch—
Who do you think'll win?
Who but a handy
Guy like Sande
Kickin' that baby in.

From "The Handy Guy" by Damon Runyon

They say that in racing things have a way of evening up. If Sande's luck was poor in 1924, it was great at Churchill Downs in 1925. The heavens opened up and the track turned to slop, which Flying Ebony loved. As with Zev, Sande put Flying Ebony on the lead from his number 6 post position.

A colt named Captain Hal immediately joined Flying Ebony, and the two were still head-and-head at the furlong pole, with Flying Ebony enjoying the slightest of advantages. At the wire it was Flying Ebony by a length and a half over Captain Hal, and everyone was in agreement that Sande, the Handy Guy, made the difference.

The Fox of Belair

Sande's constant dieting brought on stomach problems, and in the fall of 1928 he retired to train horses. He spent his own money and put together a small stable.

His victories were too few, however, and in the fall of 1929 he had to sell most of his horses. Luckily, in the winter of 1930 he was approached by the most powerful man in American racing, William Woodward, Sr., chairman of the Jockey Club and owner of Belair Stud. His good 2-year-old colt Gallant Fox had won only twice that year in seven starts. For the colt's 3-year-season Woodward wanted the best, and to him that meant Sande.

Instead of entrusting the matter to his trainer, Sunny Jim Fitzsimmons, Woodward undertook the assignment of getting Sande himself. He approached Sande to ride Gallant Fox and the two men struck a bargain.

It was a happy arrangement. With Sande up, Gallant Fox won the Wood Memorial and the Preakness. Next the partners traveled to Churchill Downs for the 56th Kentucky Derby, and Gallant Fox was a solid favorite. In close quarters from post position 7 for the first half mile, Gallant Fox shook loose and Sande promptly put him on the lead, which he held, winning by two lengths from Audley

Eddie Arcaro and James Fitzsimmons

Farm's Gallant Knight. This was Sande's third Derby triumph.

The Fox of Belair went on to capture the Belmont Stakes, giving him a sweep of the Triple Crown, and also won the Dwyer Stakes, the Arlington Classic, the Saratoga Cup, the Lawrence Realization, and the Jockey Club Gold Cup. He had a brilliant season with nine victories from ten starts.

Sande's weight problems in the following years again prompted him to retire, and he began training for Maxwell Howard. In 1938 Sande was the leading money-winning trainer of the U.S., becoming the only man ever to gain that title and also to top the jockey's list in money won, which he had done on three occasions.

More than ten years after retiring, Sande again expressed the desire to ride, despite his age, and in the fall of 1953, with grim determination, he got down to riding weight. He had ten mounts, his last on October 14, 1953, when fans at Jamaica Race Track cheered as the fifty-five-year-old Sande bested Eddie Arcaro in a close finish.

The Master

A quarter of a century after his retirement, Eddie Arcaro, The Master, is still recognized as the greatest rider America ever produced. He was also the smartest and one of the strongest, and both of these qualities contributed immeasurably to his long list of achievements.

He was what the old-timers called a Main Force rider. His strength enabled him to push many a reluctant horse across the wire first, and because he was an outstanding athlete, he looked a picture in the saddle. His flat back paralleled that of his mount, his head was buried in the mane with only those piercing eyes visible, and his hands, in rhythm with the horse's stride, pushed against the neck so forcefully as to transmit the message that nothing but the horse's best effort would be accepted. And if he found any reluctance, one hand snaked out to deliver a stinging crack of the whip.

In thirty-one tempestuous seasons, he rode 4,779

winners and his mounts earned $30,039,543. Through much of Arcaro's career the opportunities to ride were only a fraction of what they are today. Despite this, he still ranks among the top ten winners.

Arcaro's record in the Triple Crown is without parallel; he won it in 1941 with Whirlaway and in 1948 with Citation. In addition to his five Kentucky Derby wins, a record he shares with Bill Hartack, he has a record six victories in the Preakness, and six victories in the Belmont Stakes, a record he shares with Jimmy McLaughlin.

But the components of his fame are much more substantial than mere statistics. By virtue of his gregarious nature, his warm personality, and his ability to articulate the ways of riding and racing, he was the focal point of the sport for many years. He was admired and respected, and his every nuance was copied slavishly. It was Arcaro more than anyone who made the acey-deucy style the norm in American riding, with the right stirrup short and the left iron long. There was opposition to the Caliente safety helmet until Arcaro began to wear it regularly.

Five Derby Victories

Arcaro was just nineteen years old when trainer Bert Williams gave him his first Kentucky Derby ride in 1935, aboard the favorite, Calumet Farm's Nellie Flag. The filly finished fourth. Three years after that Derby debut, Arcaro was signed as a contract rider by Greentree Stable. However, since Greentree had no horse for the 1938 Derby, Arcaro was given permission to ride the 8–1 Lawrin for Ben Jones and Woolford Farm. Lawrin was Arcaro's first Derby winner. Though he rode four more winners, to this day he says the thrill of that first Derby victory was the greatest of all.

A Year of Reflection

In those pre-World War II days, before the advent of the film patrol, riding was a good deal rougher than today. Violence was in vogue wherever the stewards were not tougher than the riders, and Arcaro was as volatile as any of them. In 1942, riding in New York, Arcaro thought he was abused one afternoon, coming out of the gate, by the Cuban rider Vincent Nodarse. He quickly brought his mount alongside Nodarse, jammed him into the inside rail, and sent him flying into the infield. "What were you trying to do?" the stewards asked Arcaro.

"Kill the son of a bitch," Eddie said.

Arcaro was suspended indefinitely. He worked and lived almost a year as an employee at Greentree Farm before his license was restored, late in 1943, at the special request of a letter from a dying Mrs. Payne Whitney of Greentree to Jockey Club chairman William Woodward, Sr.

During that year of banishment, Arcaro waxed reflective and gained control of his emotions. He returned to the track a more responsible man, and, as his career flourished, so did his stature.

Ballroom Negotiations

Arcaro's willingness to use his own judgment and accept responsibility may have been best illustrated in the 1952 Derby, when he rode Hill Gail for Calumet Farm. The Bull Lea colt was a wild one, and Eddie knew he could explode at any time. Leaving the backstretch, Arcaro felt Hill Gail prepare to bolt on the turn. Seizing the initiative, Arcaro set him to running.

Hill Gail opened a five-length lead in little more than a furlong, much earlier in the race than was considered wise, and the crowd gasped. Arcaro kept hammering at Hill Gail, never giving him the chance to think about a thing except running, and the big colt staggered home, exhausted but the winner by two lengths.

Arcaro, who has always lived life to the hilt, had landed the mount on Hill Gail through his own efforts. That spring he rode the imported Windy City II in the Santa Anita Derby, while Ted Atkinson, one of the country's leading jockeys, was

Eddie Arcaro and Ted Atkinson

on Hill Gail. Windy City II broke down in the race, and Hill Gail came on to win. With Windy City II injured, Arcaro suddenly had no Kentucky Derby mount.

That evening there was a ball at Santa Anita that many jockeys missed so they could be at work early the next morning. Not Eddie Arcaro. He danced with Hill Gail's owner, Lucille Markey, and told her that he was available for the Kentucky Derby and would give her first call. She promptly accepted. "The next morning," Arcaro said, "Atkinson phoned me and said he had just called Mrs. Markey, and she told him that I had been hired to ride Hill Gail in the Derby. 'Ted,' I told him, 'you should have gone to the ball.' "

The Greatest Derby Rider

While Arcaro was undoubtedly the greatest American jockey, Bill Hartack was the greatest Kentucky Derby rider of them all. In his first nine attempts Hartack rode five Kentucky Derby winners while Arcaro had to ride in thirteen Derbys to achieve his record five winners. Even more significant, Hartack was usually not on the best horse in the field. It seems safe to say that he was the key to victory with Iron Liege in 1957, with Venetian Way in 1960, with Decidedly in 1962, with Northern Dancer in 1964, and with Majestic Prince in 1969.

Arcaro himself admits that there were at least two Derbys he should have won. The only Derby for which Hartack might be faulted was the 1956 running, when, as a relatively inexperienced jockey, he might have moved a little too soon with Fabius, who was beaten by less than a length by Needles. Hartack was a quick study, however, and never again made a mistake in the Derby. Rather, with his great self-confidence and his intuitive psychological understanding of man and horse, he forced other jockeys to make mistakes and benefited from them.

He was one of the cleanest riders that ever rode, as well as one of the very best. He received very few

suspensions during his career for riding tactics (although he was suspended on several notable occasions for his demeanor and churlishness). He scrupulously avoided putting his fellow riders in peril. And unlike some of his prominent colleagues, Hartack was never one to constantly skirt the fine line between "race riding" and rough riding.

Hartack quickly rose to prominence, and in 1955, his third year of racing, with 417 winners, he was America's champion jockey. He repeated as champion in 1956 with 347 winners, when his horses set a record for earnings of $2,343,955, and he gained a third consecutive riding title in 1957 with 341 winners. Those three riding titles were without parallel until Pat Day duplicated the feat in 1982, 1983, and 1984.

Veteran racing men accustomed to Arcaro's classic seat were amazed by the success of Hartack, who appeared to bounce in the saddle rather than remain motionless or rock slightly with a horse's stride. He was constantly busy in the saddle, seeking a response from his mounts. If one tactic didn't work, he tried another. He didn't want horses to gallop along easily. He wanted them to run fast and win.

Derby Drama

In 1956 he became associated with Calumet Farm, then America's premier stable. He had his first Kentucky Derby winner the following year. Riding the second-string Iron Liege, he beat the greatest field in Kentucky Derby history under dramatic circumstances. In all the theatrical hoopla over Bill Shoemaker standing in the irons on Gallant Man, however, it should not be overlooked that Hartack put Iron Liege into a fierce drive through the stretch and refused to let his colt surrender. Iron Liege prevailed by a nose in the 83rd Derby.

A Classic Ride

Hartack had his second Kentucky Derby winner in 1960 aboard Sunny Blue Farm's Venetian Way, a Royal Coinage colt out of Firefly, bred in Kentucky by John Greathouse and trained by Vic Sovinski.

Eddie Arcaro

A runner from the outset, Venetian Way broke his maiden in his first start in February of his 2-year-old season at Hialeah. That summer he developed nicely in Chicago and won the Washington Park Futurity over the rapid Bally Ache. Venetian Way had a stifle problem, however, and Sovinski decided to put him away for the remainder of the season. The following spring Sovinski called on Hartack to ride Venetian Way in the Florida Derby. The colt ran a big race, ending up second by a nose to Bally Ache in excellent time.

The rivals met again at Churchill Downs a week before the Derby in the seven-furlong Stepping Stone Purse. Bally Ache was a decisive winner this time, which sent him into the 86th Run for the Roses as the 17–10 second choice behind the Santa Anita Derby winner, Tompion, favored at 11–10. Venetian Way was a mildly regarded 6–1.

As Venetian Way's stifles continued to bother him during Derby Week, Sovinski employed an anti-inflammatory medication to give the colt the freedom of movement he needed.

Bally Ache set the pace in that Kentucky Derby of 1960 but Venetian Way, freed at last of pain, was always close by under Hartack. It was a classic ride. Venetian Way began to put pressure on Bally Ache leaving the five-sixteenths pole, had the lead at the head of the stretch, and was two lengths in front at the eighth pole. He drew off to score by 3½ lengths, with Bally Ache second.

Luck with Luro

In the 1962 Kentucky Derby Hartack was back, aboard George Pope's Decidedly, trained by Horatio Luro. In their first collaboration at Keeneland in mid-April, Hartack rode Decidedly to a second-place finish.

Encouraged, Luro "turned the screws" a little for the subsequent Blue Grass Stakes, and, again following orders to the letter, Hartack brought Decidedly from off the pace to finish second to Ridan, who went into the Kentucky Derby as the 11–10 favorite.

It was a Derby full of speed, and Decidedly's only chance was to come from behind and let the speed horses race one another into submission. But these tactics called for a good deal of self-control on the part of the rider. The leaders raced the first mile in a crisp 1:35⅕, with Decidedly far back. Then Hartack brought the gray colt on and won by a decisive 2¼ lengths, setting a track record of 2:00⅖.

In 1964 Horatio Luro had another top colt in Windfields Farm's Northern Dancer. But his regular jockey, Bill Shoemaker, was unimpressed, despite victories in the Flamingo and Florida Derby, and decided to ride Santa Anita Derby winner Hill Rise in the Kentucky Derby. Hartack was chosen as Shoe's successor.

In a field of twelve for the 90th Kentucky Derby, Hill Rise was the 7–5 favorite. Northern Dancer, who won the Blue Grass Stakes, was second choice at 3–1 in a confrontation that was billed as the Good Big Horse against the Good Little Horse.

Hill Rise and Northern Dancer came away leisurely at the start. Turning into the backstretch, Hill Rise was on the outside and Northern Dancer was on the inside behind a wall of horses. Shoemaker, aware of the threat from Northern Dancer, moved to box him in, but Hartack anticipated the move a split second earlier and angled to the outside.

Hartack sent his mount into the clear and went on about his business. As the crowd roared, Hill Rise swept after The Dancer and was slowly getting to him when he ran out of furlongs. The margin was a neck, and Northern Dancer's winning time was a record 2:00.

A Majestic Victory

Hartack's career began to turn soon thereafter. His relations with some important stables had deteriorated, and he was getting on fewer good horses. After four Derby victories Hartack's expertise was unquestioned, but his abrasive personality had become a problem.

Not to Johnny Longden, however. The Hall of Fame

jockey, a born horseman, had begun working with a terrific 2-year-old prospect in 1968, a $250,000 yearling purchase by Raise a Native out of Gay Hostess by Royal Charger. His name was Majestic Prince.

Because of his sales price, a tremendous sum at the time, Majestic Prince was a celebrity from the outset. He won his first race by almost three lengths. Leading all the way under Hartack, it was an auspicious debut. By Derby Day he had won his next six straight races.

The Kentucky Derby, on May 3, drew a strong field of eight, with Majestic Prince the 7–5 favorite. A 28–1 outsider named Ocean Roar set the pace, with Top Knight, Arts and Letters, and Majestic Prince following behind as the second flight. On the far turn Arts and Letters was ahead, with Majestic Prince close behind. With three furlongs remaining, Hartack asked Majestic Prince to run and took the lead away from Arts and Letters turning into the stretch.

Braulio Baeza on Arts and Letters quickly roused his colt and came on to challenge Majestic Prince, but the damage had been done. Majestic Prince had half a length on Arts and Letters at the furlong pole, and although the challenger persisted in his bid and succeeded in narrowing the margin to a neck at the wire, he could not catch the courageous Prince.

Longden became the only individual to both ride a Kentucky Derby winner (Count Fleet) and train one (Majestic Prince), and Hartack equaled Eddie Arcaro's record of having ridden five winners of the Kentucky Derby.

With his business almost at a standstill at home in 1974, Hartack signed a contract with the Royal Hong Kong Jockey Club and became a regular at the quaint Happy Valley track for six years.

In the winter of 1980, when he was forty-seven, Hartack injured an ankle and retired from the saddle. Returning to the States, he served as a racing official and as a television commentator for the Triple Crown races. His insightful remarks

Bill Hartack (1A) on Iron Liege and Bill Shoemaker (5) up in the irons on Gallant Man in 1957—a dream comes true

Jockey	Time	Year	Horse
Ron Turcotte	1:59 2/5	1973	Secretariat
Bill Hartack	2:00	1964	Northern Dancer
Angel Cordero, Jr.	2:00 1/5	1985	Spend a Buck
Bill Hartack	2:00 2/5	1962	Decidedly
Bobby Ussery	2:00 3/5	1967	Proud Clarion
Bill Shoemaker	2:01 1/5	1965	Lucky Debonair
Steve Cauthen	2:01 1/5	1978	Affirmed
Eddie Arcaro	2:01 2/5	1941	Whirlaway
William Boland	2:01 3/5	1950	Middleground
Eddie Arcaro	2:01 3/5	1952	Hill Gail
Angel Cordero, Jr.	2:01 3/5	1976	Bold Forbes

Fastest Runnings

Jockey	Time	Year	Horse
Eddie Arcaro	2:04 4/5	1938	Lawrin
	2:01 2/5	1941	Whirlaway
	2:07	1945	Hoop Jr.
	2:05 2/5	1948	Citation
	2:01 3/5	1952	Hill Gail
Bill Hartack	2:02 1/5	1957	Iron Liege
	2:02 2/5	1960	Venetian Way
	2:00 2/5	1962	Decidedly
	2:00	1964	Northern Dancer
	2:01 4/5	1969	Majestic Prince
Bill Shoemaker	2:01 4/5	1955	Swaps
	2:02 1/5	1959	Tomy Lee
	2:01 1/5	1965	Lucky Debonair
	2:02 4/5	1986	Ferdinand
Isaac Murphy	2:40 1/4	1884	Buchanan
	2:45	1890	Riley
	2:52 1/4	1891	Kingman
Earl Sande	2:05 2/5	1923	Zev
	2:07 3/5	1925	Flying Ebony
	2:07 3/5	1930	Gallant Fox
Angel Cordero, Jr.	2:04	1974	Cannonade
	2:01 3/5	1976	Bold Forbes
	2:00 1/5	1985	Spend a Buck

Most Wins

Bill Hartack, 1969

were hailed as among the most knowledgeable and provocative ever offered on a racing program.

But it was as a rider that he had gained his greatest fame. In twenty-two seasons in the U.S. he rode 4,272 winners, who earned $26,466,758. In 1959, only seven years after he rode his first race at Waterford Park, he was elected to the Racing Hall of Fame in Saratoga Springs, New York. No other jockey has been honored so quickly, but then, none has tried harder to win every race in which he rode.

The Angel from Santurce

He is at once Liberace and Mac the Knife, charming owners in the paddock with the warmest smile in racing and then permitting his horse to drift on the stretch turn, carrying out of contention the horse trained by a man who no longer gives him winning mounts. Whether in beatific or vengeful mode, or when he is at work through the stretch, driving his horse to the wire like a man possessed, his motivation is always the same. He is indeed possessed, and the demon does business as Victory.

Racing offers the public wagering options of win, place, and show. Angel Cordero, Jr., recognizes only the win, and few, if any, have done it better. With over 6,000 winners, he is the third-winningest jockey in racing history; only Bill Shoemaker, with some 8,700 winners, and Laffit Pincay, Jr., with some 6,800 winners, surpass his total. Cordero has ridden the winners of more than $110 million in purses, making him second only to Pincay's $112 million on the all-time earners' list. At the prestigious Saratoga race meeting he was the leading rider for a record eleven consecutive years. He was America's leading jockey in 1968, with 345 winners, and the country's leading money-winning rider four times, in 1976, 1982, 1983, and 1987. Cordero has ridden three Kentucky Derby winners, and his performances on Cannonade in 1974, Bold Forbes in 1976, and Spend a Buck in 1985 bordered on the spectacular.

When it comes to crossing the line between "race riding"—the skill of the professional in seeking an advantage up to the limit of the rules—and rough riding, Cordero's record is splattered with over 200 suspensions in a career that began in 1960. Most of those suspensions, he says, were for trying too hard to win. Trainers have come to realize that Cordero is a tremendous asset riding for them and a dangerous opponent.

He is keenly intelligent and informed about all matters to do with racing. He is much closer to horses and their psyches than the average jockey, knows every aspect of his profession as a rider, and is an excellent handicapper in evaluating the quality of a horse. He is also a sharp amateur psychiatrist and keeps a mental "book" on all leading jockeys, enabling him to anticipate their actions under certain conditions.

Cordero's intensity is contrasted by his public persona, that of a Child of Joy. He is constantly moving, smiling, and singing in Spanish. He seems to love horses and is often seen stroking them fondly. He also gives the fans a show, smiling and exchanging comments on his way to the track and then, in victory, frequently springing in the air out of his stirrups and landing on the ground like an acrobat, in a fashion made famous in Canada some years earlier by the late, great Avelino Gomez.

Cordero is very generous of his time and attention. He visits sick children in hospitals, attends fund-raising dinners, helps young jockeys with advice, is remarkably accessible to the media for interviews, and is the soul of graciousness and charm to one and all.

Born in Santurce, Puerto Rico, the son of a jockey and trainer, Cordero had his first Kentucky Derby ride in 1968, and although he finished thirteenth in a field of fourteen aboard Elmendorf Farm's Verbatim, he became intrigued with the Derby.

A Chinese Fire Drill

For the Derby of 1974, Cordero landed the mount on John M. Olin's Cannonade. The centennial field

Angel Cordero, Jr., 1976

268

numbered a record twenty-three, with Woody Stephens's entry of Judger and Cannonade favored at 3–2. Judger, winner of the Florida Derby and Blue Grass Stakes, appeared the stronger half of the entry under Laffit Pincay, Jr.

Under a positively brilliant performance by Cordero, Cannonade won by 2¼ lengths. The large field spelled ruination for most of the horses with a chance to win, such as Judger and Little Current. Judger was squeezed back at the start and lost all chance immediately, while Little Current's jockey, Bob Ussery, was forced to check five times during the race, which resembled a Chinese fire drill.

Cannonade did not have a problem-free race. He was roughed at the start, but Cordero patiently permitted many of his opponents to pass him and then picked his way in heavy traffic like a broken-field runner in football. After improving his position steadily on the outside, Cordero moved Cannonade to the inside on the final turn and quickly opened up a substantial lead at the furlong pole. Cannonade held on nicely to win while some of the other favorites tired badly in the drive.

The Puerto Rican Speedball

Cordero's second Kentucky Derby victory came two years later with Bold Forbes. A wonder horse as a 2-year-old, when he won seven of eight starts, Bold Forbes raced for a San Juan sportsman, Enrique Rodriquez Tizol. The States-bred colt by Irish Castle out of Comely Nell had plenty of breeding, but his Puerto Rican racing background prompted many American experts to hold him in light regard. When owner Rodriquez Tizol decided to send Bold Forbes to the States for his 3-year-old racing—he had run out of competition in Puerto Rico—he put in a call to an old friend, Laz Barrera.

A colt of blazing speed, Bold Forbes had stamina limitations, which trainer Barrera initially addressed through a series of long, slow gallops. Barrera knew what he was doing, and so did Cordero.

Honest Pleasure, the 2–5 favorite for the 102nd Kentucky Derby, was also a colt of extreme speed, and he and Bold Forbes could easily have run each other into the ground if they had gone head-and-head. In the Derby, however, Cordero cleverly got the lead he so desperately wanted, and then, before Braulio Baeza on Honest Pleasure could compose himself, he opened a five-length advantage. Steadily, Honest Pleasure whittled away at Bold Forbes's lead, but always with Cordero's concurrence. Angel so skillfully saved his reserve that Bold Forbes won by a length. It was a tour de force for trainer and jockey.

No One Catches Cordero

Cordero's third Kentucky Derby victory, in 1985 with Spend a Buck, was another masterpiece of a different style. By every aspect of race analysis the two outstanding speed horses, Spend a Buck and Eternal Prince, should have burned each other out. The difference, of course, was an Angel.

It was the experienced Cordero on Spend a Buck and the relatively inexperienced Richard Migliore on Eternal Prince. Migliore's first appearance in the Run for the Roses was exciting enough, but for the young New Yorker to be on a horse given a chance to win by some handicappers made the tension even greater for him.

Cordero added fuel to the fire with several informal conversations—"psych jobs" in the trade—and Migliore was as tight as a stretched wire when he entered the starting gate aboard Eternal Prince. In Kentucky, when the last horse is loaded, the starter traditionally springs the latch immediately. In some other jurisdictions there is a pause for the horses to settle themselves and for the riders to prepare mentally for the break. Veteran riders expect a sudden start in the Derby.

When the starting gates opened for the 111th Run for the Roses, Cordero got Spend a Buck out of his stall like a scalded cat, while Eternal Prince and Migliore were in repose. They came out tardily and the race was over in the first two strides. By the

Angel Cordero, Jr., 1974

first turn, Spend a Buck enjoyed an advantage of five lengths on his closest pursuer, and that was it. No one was going to catch Spend a Buck that day.

Chalk up another for Angel. He may hang up his halo in the jockey's room before a race, but he never takes off his wings.

Shoemaker's Mark

Every sport has a record that will never be broken. In racing, the mark of marks is held by Bill Shoemaker, who has ridden some 8,700 winners. For a jockey, riding 200 winners a year is a big season, and only about 30 of some 3,000 riders at North American tracks each year will ride that many victors. If a jockey were to win 200 races a year for forty years, he would still not catch Shoemaker.

Shoemaker has won four Kentucky Derbys and has ridden in a record twenty-five, and he probably should have also won several others, among them the 1957 Derby aboard Gallant Man—in which he misjudged the finish line, standing in the irons prematurely.

A Great Ride from the Little Man

In 1955, however, Shoe did everything right. Nashua, perhaps the soundest and one of the most talented horses of the century, was a heavy favorite for the 81st Kentucky Derby. With The Master, Eddie Arcaro, in the irons, the colt had trained smartly for the Derby under the supervision of Sunny Jim Fitzsimmons. Nashua went on to capture the Preakness and the Belmont Stakes, but was upset as a 13–10 choice in the Run for the Roses. Shoe rode Swaps, by Khaled out of Iron Reward, a colt owned and bred by rancher Rex Ellsworth. The rangy chestnut was trained in California by Mesh Tenney. As a tune-up for the Kentucky Derby, Tenney ran Swaps in a six-furlong allowance a week prior to the Derby. With Shoemaker up, Swaps won by 8½ lengths. Even so, Swaps failed to impress easterners.

"He beat nothing, he's trained by a cowboy, and he has no chance against a colt with the class of Nashua."

Swaps went to the lead early on in the Derby but Arcaro, on Nashua, was not interested. Instead he had his eye on Summer Tan, who had given Nashua a hard race in the Wood Memorial. Nashua, always well placed by Arcaro, went from third to second at the head of the stretch, and the large crowd expected him to pass Swaps easily. The two colts were only half a length apart at the furlong pole, but Shoemaker was prepared. When Arcaro applied pressure with Nashua, Shoemaker met the challenge and drove Swaps home a conclusive winner by a length and a half.

"The best horse won," Arcaro said later with typical frankness. "He got a great ride from the Little Man, who always has something left."

Beware of Tomy Lee

Shoemaker's second Derby victory came four years later in 1959 with an English-bred colt named Tomy Lee, owned by a Midland, Texas, oil man named Fred Turner, Jr., and trained by seventy-one-year-old Frank Childs.

A top 2-year-old, Tomy Lee finished second in the Champagne Stakes at Belmont Park but was disqualified and placed third for bearing out, a bad habit he had. No one wanted to be on the outside of Tomy Lee.

Troilus, the Flamingo winner, set the pace in the Derby, with Tomy Lee second and Sword Dancer with Bill Boland up, a well-placed fourth. At the half-mile pole Tomy Lee and Sword Dancer both began to duel for the lead, with Sword Dancer taking command after entering the stretch. That looked like a decisive move, and Shoemaker, always a sport, called out to Boland, "Good luck and win it."

Shoe was having his problems at that point, for Tomy Lee had not changed leads going from the turn to the straight. To avoid fatigue, horses are supposed to lead with their right leg on the

straightaway and their left leg on the turns. Before Shoe could get Tomy Lee to change leads, the colt drifted out, eventually brushing with Sword Dancer, who raced wide into the stretch. This action seemed to anger Sword Dancer, who began to lug in on Tomy Lee. Tomy Lee drifted again, and the two colts bumped several times, with Sword Dancer apparently the principal aggressor from the outside. On one of their final collisions, Sword Dancer did Tomy Lee a big favor. He bumped him onto the correct lead. Tomy Lee immediately spurted forward and beat Sword Dancer by a nose at the post.

Boland lodged a claim of foul, one of the very few such claims in Kentucky Derby history, alleging that Sword Dancer had been carried wide by Tomy Lee around the far turn and through the upper stretch. However, the stewards, after studying the film patrol, permitted the numbers to stand. In retrospect, Boland had put himself in harm's way. He had failed to heed the adage: Don't be outside of Tomy Lee.

Ready to Run

Shoemaker's third Kentucky Derby triumph came in 1965 aboard Lucky Debonair. The homebred colt by Vertex was owned by Dan and Ada Rice of Wheaton, Illinois, and trained by former jockey Frank Catrone.

The 91st Kentucky Derby of 1965 drew a field of eleven without a real standout. Lucky Debonair, third choice for the Derby, was moderately sized but attractive. With his arrival in Kentucky, he began to bloom for Catrone. He made steady progress and had a particularly good seven-furlong move of 1:25⅕ four days prior to the Derby. When Shoe got off him that morning, he turned to Catrone and said quietly, "He's ready."

Flag Raiser, the front-running winner of the Wood Memorial, set the pace in the Derby, but Lucky Debonair was not far off him and drew abreast on the backstretch. These two staged a pretty duel to the quarter-pole, at which point Shoe asked Lucky

Debonair to run. In a twinkling, he opened a three-length advantage and won the Derby by a neck over the fast-closing Dapper Dan.

The Oldest Derby Winner

Shoe was thirty-three when he rode Lucky Debonair to victory. He was fifty-four when he returned to the winner's circle at Churchill Downs, in 1986, aboard Ferdinand.

A beautifully bred son of the great racehorse and sire Nijinsky II, Ferdinand was owned and bred by the Howard Kecks of California and trained by Hall of Famer Charlie Whittingham. Whittingham knew that as a horse of some size, Ferdinand would take a while to get his act together. So he was not concerned that it took Ferdinand four races to break his maiden with Shoemaker up.

At 3, Ferdinand kept knocking at the door all winter in California, posting a win and two close seconds in stakes races before losing some stature by finishing a distant third in the Santa Anita Derby. Whittingham brought him to Churchill Downs earlier than is customary and Ferdinand began to train very well over the historic Downs track. When the colt went a mile in 1:38⅘, Whittingham knew he had a good chance.

Despite his good form and penchant for the Churchill Downs track, Ferdinand was not everyone's choice for the 112th Kentucky Derby. Ferdinand was more or less dismissed at 18–1.

A genuine speedster named Groovy led for the first six furlongs. Ferdinand, last of sixteen starters at one point, was still far back in the field when Groovy ran out of steam and Broad Brush, Badger Land, and Bold Arrangement moved into the stretch as the leaders. Ferdinand moved quickly at this point, splitting horses in the upper stretch, only to face another wall of horses in front of him.

It was a classic situation, with Shoemaker forced to make a difficult decision in a split second. Should he go to the outside and lose considerable ground? Just then, a smaller hole opened along the rail. Shoe did not waste a second in heading for the narrow

opening. Pat Day on Rampage hesitated an instant in going for the same opening. Only Shoe and Ferdinand got through. The hole closed as quickly as it had opened.

Once through, Ferdinand broke the race open with a flourish and won the Derby by 2¼ lengths from the English colt Bold Arrangement. Shoemaker became the oldest rider ever to win this prize of prizes.

What makes him the Shoe? Along with great athletic ability, excellent balance, and intelligence, Shoe's disposition has been another factor in his success. Those who know him are unanimous in the assessment that he is the most even-tempered individual they have ever met, perpetually serene and apparently happy. He has an excellent sense of humor, is a good conversationalist, and has a keen sense of where he is going without hitting you over the head with his opinion.

How long will he ride? As long as he can get on good horses and do them justice, he has said on many occasions. He was one of the country's leading jockeys in 1986, when he rode the winners of more than $7 million in purses, and had another fine season in 1987 with almost $7 million.

The Kentucky Derby is horse racing's Super Bowl and World Series, one of those rare happenings in which everyone has an interest, layman as well as expert. As an athletic contest, maybe it comes too soon and asks horses too young to run too far. If anything, it is the first measure of greatness in a horse, not the last.

Trainer Jack Van Berg worked the small tracks for decades to build a reputation as a solid horseman who could take common runners and make them winners. He had 5000 horses before he brought Alysheba to Louisville, but in four tries he hadn't won a Derby. With Alysheba, he said, "I thought we'd win if The Man Above was with us, and He was."

Chris McCarron, like thousands of big little men in this century and the last, first rode a racehorse with one dream—winning the Derby. National riding champion and winner of more than 4,600 races, he had never captured the Derby. Five months before he rode Alysheba in the 1987 Derby, Chris McCarron rode in a wheelchair, the femur of his left leg splintered in four places from when a horse fell with him at Santa Anita. He had been back to work only six weeks before coming to Louisville with Alysheba for the race horsemen use as the measure of their worth. Yet even after Alysheba's stumble in the stretch and the tragedy it portended, McCarron said he never thought of being hurt. He only wanted to win.

"A guy's lucky if he gets to ride in one Derby ever," McCarron said after winning. "And to do this, it's a dream. I'm trembling."

1986 Ferdinand, Bill Shoemaker

1985 Spend a Buck, Angel Cordero, Jr.

1982 Gato Del Sol, Eddie Delahoussaye

1981 Pleasant Colony, Jorge Velasquez

1977 Seattle Slew, Jean Cruguet

1974 Cannonade, Angel Cordero, Jr.

1971 Canonero II, Gustavo Avila

1969 Majestic Prince, Bill Hartack

1984 Swale, Laffit Pincay, Jr.

1983 Sunny's Halo, Eddie Delahoussaye

1979 Spectacular Bid, Ronald Franklin

1978 Affirmed, Steve Cauthen

1973 Secretariat, Ron Turcotte

1972 Riva Ridge, Ron Turcotte

1967 Proud Clarion, Bobby Ussery

1960 Venetian Way, Bill Hartack

1984 Laffit Pincay, Jr.

1966 Don Brumfield

1985 Angel Cordero, Jr.

1978 Steve Cauthen

1981 Jorge Velasquez

1969 Bill Hartack

1971 Gustavo Avila

1975 Jacinto Vasquez

When Peter Fuller came to Louisville in 1968 with his colt Dancer's Image, the Boston automobile dealer and sportsman was so confident he said, "We're going to win it. . . . I know the Derby is made for this horse."

Early Derby Week, Fuller practiced walking from his seat to the winner's circle. He wanted to find the quickest route out of the grandstand, across the track, and to the presentation stand. On Derby Day, he did in fact make that happy walk. Ironically, two years later, Fuller had to give back the trophy after his colt was disqualified for taking medication. The first place purse and trophy were awarded to Calumet Farm.

They drape a blanket of roses over the colt's shoulders. They hand the jockey a dozen roses of his own. They paint the colt's name in gold in a gallery of champions over a century in the making. From Aristides to Sir Barton to Citation to Secretariat to Alysheba, the line of immortality runs with the strength and beauty of great poetry.

In 1987 the trainer Jack Van Berg, a garrulous man, took his trophy and began to speak. He wept instead. Composing himself at last, he said, "I don't remember ever feeling this way before."

Authors

Joe Hirsch has worked for the *Daily Racing Form* for the last forty years; his daily column is read by racing enthusiasts across North America. An authority on the Triple Crown Classics, Hirsch has won numerous writing awards, including the Walter Haight Award of the National Turf Writers Association for a long and distinguished career. In addition, he is the only American writer to receive the Lord Derby Award from the English Horse Racing Writers Association, bestowed for his encouragement of international racing.

Jim Bolus is the communications director of the Kentucky Thoroughbred Association and the Thoroughbred Owners and Breeders Association. As a Louisville newspaperman, Bolus covered the Kentucky Derby for over twenty years, and he is the author of *Run for the Roses*, a history of the Derby. He has won seven national awards for his writing, and is a leading authority on the Derby's rich history.

Dave Kindred, author of the caption essay, is a renowned sports columnist for *The Atlanta Constitution*. He has reported sports events around the world, and has covered the last twenty-two Derbys. Kindred won the prestigious 1981 Eclipse Award—the highest honor in thoroughbred horse-racing journalism—and in 1987 he received the Associated Press Sports Editors Award as the best sports columnist in America. He is the author of three books on sports subjects.

Contributing Photographers

Jerry Cooke is a distinguished photographer of international horse racing. He has covered thirty-two consecutive Kentucky Derbys for *Sports Illustrated*, and more of his Derby photographs have appeared on that magazine's covers than those of any other photographer. Many of Cooke's pictures are on permanent exhibit in the newly renovated National Museum of Racing and Hall of Fame in Saratoga Springs, New York.

Donna Lawrence Productions, Inc., is a Louisville-based audio-visual production company recognized as a leader in the field of multi-image and video presentations. The company's "The Greatest Race: A Kentucky Derby Panorama, " a permanent multi-media exhibit housed in the Kentucky Derby Museum, has won numerous awards.

Michael Brohm, a prize-winning commercial photographer, specializes in horse-racing pictures. He has contributed to several multi-media exhibits on horse-racing, including Donna Lawrence's production, "The Greatest Race." His work has been exhibited at the Nikon House Gallery in New York.

Scott Goldsmith is a free-lance photographer who has covered the last ten Kentucky Derbys. He has received awards for his work, which has appeared in many major publications, including *National Geographic* and *Time*. His photographs of Churchill Downs have been shown at the Nikon House Gallery.

This chart lists winners for the last four decades. In 1968 Dancer's Image won, but was later disqualified, and Forward Pass was named the victor.

Year	Winner	Jockey	Time	Track
1950	Middleground	W. Boland	2:01 3/5	Fast
1951	Count Turf	C. McCreary	2:02 3/5	Fast
1952	Hill Gail	E. Arcaro	2:01 3/5	Fast
1953	Dark Star	H. Moreno	2:02	Fast
1954	Determine	R. York	2:03	Fast
1955	Swaps	W. Shoemaker	2:01 4/5	Fast
1956	Needles	D. Erb	2:03 2/5	Fast
1957	Iron Liege	W. Hartack	2:02 1/5	Fast
1958	Tim Tam	I. Valenzuela	2:05	Muddy
1959	Tomy Lee	W. Shoemaker	2:02 1/5	Fast
1960	Venetian Way	W. Hartack	2:02 2/5	Good
1961	Carry Back	J. Sellers	2:04	Good
1962	Decidedly	W. Hartack	2:00 2/5	Fast
1963	Chateaugay	B. Baeza	2:01 4/5	Fast
1964	Northern Dancer	W. Hartack	2:00	Fast
1965	Lucky Debonair	W. Shoemaker	2:01 1/5	Fast
1966	Kauai King	D. Brumfield	2:02	Fast
1967	Proud Clarion	R. Ussery	2:00 3/5	Fast
1968	Forward Pass	I. Valenzuela	2:02 1/5	Fast
1969	Majestic Prince	W. Hartack	2:01 4/5	Fast
1970	Dust Commander	M. Manganello	2:03 2/5	Good
1971	Canonero II	G. Avila	2:03 1/5	Fast
1972	Riva Ridge	R. Turcotte	2:01 4/5	Fast
1973	Secretariat	R. Turcotte	1:59 2/5	Fast
1974	Cannonade	A. Cordero Jr.	2:04	Fast
1975	Foolish Pleasure	J. Vasquez	2:02	Fast
1976	Bold Forbes	A. Cordero Jr.	2:01 3/5	Fast
1977	Seattle Slew	J. Cruguet	2:02 1/5	Fast
1978	Affirmed	S. Cauthen	2:01 1/5	Fast
1979	Spectacular Bid	R. Franklin	2:02 2/5	Fast
1980	Genuine Risk	J. Vasquez	2:02	Fast
1981	Pleasant Colony	J. Velasquez	2:02	Fast
1982	Gato Del Sol	E. Delahoussaye	2:02 2/5	Fast
1983	Sunny's Halo	E. Delahoussaye	2:02 1/5	Fast
1984	Swale	L. Pincay Jr.	2:02 2/5	Fast
1985	Spend a Buck	A. Cordero Jr.	2:00 1/5	Fast
1986	Ferdinand	W. Shoemaker	2:02 4/5	Fast
1987	Alysheba	C.J. McCarron	2:03 2/5	Fast

Index

Numbers in regular type refer to text. Numbers in italics refer to photographs.

Chanticleer Staff
Publisher: Paul Steiner
Editor-in-Chief: Gudrun Buettner
Executive Editor: Susan Costello
Managing Editor: Jane Opper
Associate Editor: Lisa Leventer
Assistant Editor: Amy K. Hughes
Production Manager: Helga Lose
Production Assistant: Gina Stead-Thomas
Picture Librarian: Edward Douglas
Art Director: Carol Nehring
Art Associates: Ayn Svoboda, Cheryl Miller